A PRACTICAL GUIDE TO
ACCOUNT BASED MARKETING

Elevate your Brand and Drive Business Growth

Sebastian Pistritto

A PRACTICAL GUIDE TO ACCOUNT-BASED MARKETING

Copyright © 2024 Sebastian Pistritto..

All rights reserved.
No part of this book may be used or reproduced by any means, graphic, electronic, or mechanical, including photocopying, recording, taping or by any information storage retrieval system without written permission of the author except in the case of brief quotations embodied in critical articles and reviews.

Printed In: United States Of America
Published By: Hemingway Publishers

Account-Based Marketing has gained significant prominence in the Business to Business (B2B) marketing landscape, and its importance for B2B marketers cannot be overstated. Account-based marketing has many key components to it and, when executed correctly, can significantly increase brand awareness, generate more qualified leads, and grow revenues for your business. I hope this book will provide a comprehensive understanding of Account-Based Marketing, what it is, and how to implement it successfully as part of your sales and marketing efforts across the organization. My goal in this book is to detail the core areas of Account-Based Marketing, the different ways to leverage Account-Based Marketing across the different tactics of marketing, and show you the resources needed, the technology, or the tech stack that you will need to invest in. I will also discuss the processes that you will need to create and implement across your organization. The people and functional areas need to be established to have a successful and scalable demand generation for all B2B marketers.

TABLE OF CONTENTS

INTRODUCTION
    Account-Based Marketing (ABM) And Its Importance For B2b Marketers 1

CHAPTER 1
    Getting Started With Account-Based Marketing. . 4

CHAPTER 2
    Precise Targeting And Focus In B2B Account-Based Marketing (ABM) 9

CHAPTER 3
    Personalized Content And Relevance Messaging. 16

CHAPTER 4
    Digital Advertising And Account-Based Marketing 23

CHAPTER 5
    Understanding The Role Of Social Media In Account-Based Marketing 30

CHAPTER 6
    Promoting Events With Account-Based Marketing 36

CHAPTER 7
    How To Implement Webinars And Podcasts To Account-Based Marketing 44

CHAPTER 8
    Leveraging ABM In Public Relations Strategies .   50

CHAPTER 9
    Strong Sales And Marketing Alignment In B2B Account-Based Marketing   55

CHAPTER 10
    How To Mange And Improved Lead Quality . .   61

CHAPTER 11
    Managing Enhanced Customer Relationships .   67

CHAPTER 12
    How To Have Robust Return On Investment (ROI)   75

CHAPTER 13
    Building A Scalability And Adaptability Marketing Program.   81

CHAPTER 14
    Account-Based Marketing Effective In Complex Sales Cycles   88

CHAPTER 15
    How To Implement Data-Driven Decision-Making   95

CHAPTER 16
    Intent Data And Account-Based Marketing . .   101

CHAPTER 17
    Behavioral Data And How To Leverage In Account-Based Marketing   108

CHAPTER 18
    Account-Based Marketing Metrics And Analytics   113

CHAPTER 19
    Making Account-Based Marketing A Competitive Advantage 119

CHAPTER 20
    The Significance Of Buyer Personas In B2B Marketing 125

CHAPTER 21
    Tech Stack For Your Account-Based Marketing Program. 137

CHAPTER 22
    Account Based Marketing Requires A Specialized Team. 145

CHAPTER 23
    Account Based Marketing For Your Mobile Marketing Programs 150

CHAPTER 24
    Step-By-Step Guide To Implementing ABM For Email Marketing 156

CHAPTER 25
    Customer Relationship Management (CRM) System Crucial In Account-Based Marketing 163

Conclusion
    The Imperative For B2B Tech Companies To Embrace Account-Based Marketing In 2024 167

ABOUT THE AUTHOR 172
APPENDIX 175

INTRODUCTION

ACCOUNT-BASED MARKETING (ABM) AND ITS IMPORTANCE FOR B2B MARKETERS

In the world of B2B marketing, Account-Based Marketing (ABM) has emerged as a proven and strategic approach to reaching and engaging with key targeted accounts. ABM is a highly focused marketing strategy and approach that targets specific companies or accounts rather than broad demographics or industries. It involves tailoring marketing efforts to resonate with the unique needs and preferences of individual accounts. It can help to identify the marketing channels best suited for your audience. Determine the key messages, the amount of frequency, and how and when to engage to generate highly qualified leads and customers. With its focus on revenue generation or customer retention, I've found that through my own experience, ABM can help to improve lead quality, streamline sales and create customer stickiness for greater ROI. This book provides an in-depth overview of what Account-Based Marketing is and discusses its importance for your B2B marketing needs.

What Is Account-Based Marketing (ABM)

Account-Based Marketing (ABM) is a strategic approach to B2B marketing that flips the traditional lead-generation model on its head. Instead of casting a wide net to capture as many leads as possible, ABM focuses on identifying a select group of high-value accounts and tailoring marketing efforts to engage and convert those accounts. The core principle of ABM is to treat each targeted account as a market of one. and by leveraging marketing analytics, you can quickly determine if your approach is working or needs tweaking or optimization along the way.

Let's Discuss the Key Components of ABM:

- The first thing is identifying target accounts: In ABM, the first step is identifying the key accounts that align with your business goals. In other words, who is your target audience? These accounts are typically selected based on factors like industry, geographical location, number of employees, revenue size, strategic fit to your business, and the likelihood of success.
- Next, determine what is the outcome or business results that your target audience can achieve with your product or solution. Create customized content and messaging: Once target accounts are identified, the marketing team creates highly personalized content and messaging that speaks directly to the specific needs, challenges, and pain points of each account. This ensures that the content is highly relevant and engaging.
- Now think about what are the existing channels that your target audience is already utilizing to gather insights and knowledge to grow their business. Create a multichannel

approach: ABM employs a multichannel approach, utilizing various marketing channels such as email, social media, webinars, and direct outreach to reach and engage the individuals within the target accounts.
- Alignment with Sales: ABM requires close alignment between the marketing and sales teams. Sales and marketing collaborate to ensure that the messaging and outreach are coordinated and that the efforts are mutually reinforcing.
- Measurement and Analysis: ABM strategies rely on detailed measurement and analysis to evaluate the effectiveness of campaigns and make data-driven adjustments. Metrics often include engagement rates, conversion rates, and the impact on revenue.

As you begin to formulate your marketing plans, remember that Account-Based Marketing is a strategic approach, and it offers numerous advantages for B2B marketing efforts. It enables precise targeting, personalization, improved lead quality, and stronger sales and marketing alignment, leading to a better ROI and a competitive edge. With the potential for stronger customer relationships and increased revenue, ABM has become an indispensable tool for B2B marketers looking to thrive in a competitive and dynamic market. Now, let's dig deeper int the various components of Account-Based Marketing and start with how to create a framework that can support your strategic efforts, enable critical tactics, and be a robust and scalable solution.

CHAPTER 1

GETTING STARTED WITH ACCOUNT-BASED MARKETING

Creating a comprehensive framework for a B2B Account-Based Marketing (ABM) strategy is essential for achieving success. ABM involves a strategic approach that focuses on targeting high-value accounts and delivering personalized experiences. Below is an outline of the critical components to developing a strategy that we are going to build together that constitutes a robust ABM framework. We are going to look at the different components that make up the framework.

I. Strategy Development

- Define Objectives: Clearly outline your ABM goals, such as increasing revenue from key accounts, improving customer retention, or entering new markets.
- Ideal Customer Profile (ICP): Identify the characteristics of the accounts that are most valuable to your business. Factors may include industry, company size, location, and more.

- Account Selection: Use your ICP to select high-potential target accounts. Prioritize these accounts based on their alignment with your objectives.
- Stakeholder Mapping: Identify and map key decision-makers and influencers within the target accounts. Understand their roles, responsibilities, and pain points.
- Personalization Strategy: Develop a plan for tailoring content and messaging to resonate with the unique needs and challenges of each target account.

II. Data and Technology

- Data Collection: Set up data collection processes to gather information on target accounts, including firmographics, intent data, and historical data.
- CRM and Marketing Automation: Implement or optimize your CRM system and marketing automation tools to manage, track, and analyze data for ABM.
- Data Integration: Integrate data from various sources to create a unified view of target accounts. This may include data from CRM, marketing automation, and third-party providers.
- Analytics and Reporting: Establish metrics and key performance indicators (KPIs) to measure the success of your ABM campaigns. Use analytics to track performance and provide actionable insights.
- Personalization Tools: Invest in tools that facilitate content personalization, such as dynamic content generators and personalization platforms.

III. Campaign Execution

- Content Creation: Develop highly customized content that directly addresses the needs and interests of each target account. This includes whitepapers, case studies, webinars, and more.
- Multi-Channel Outreach: Utilize various channels for engagement, such as email, social media, webinars, personalized landing pages, and direct mail, to ensure consistent messaging.
- Account-Based Advertising: Implement paid advertising campaigns that target specific accounts or segments, ensuring that your message reaches the right audience.
- Nurture and Engagement: Plan a sequence of engagements that nurture target accounts and guide them through the buyer's journey, delivering valuable content at each stage.
- Personalized Email Campaigns: Create highly personalized email campaigns that speak directly to the account's needs and challenges. Leverage marketing automation for timely and relevant communications.

IV. Measurement and Optimization

- Lead Scoring: Develop lead scoring models that identify the readiness of leads within target accounts to progress through the sales funnel.
- Conversion Tracking: Implement tools to track conversions and measure the impact of ABM campaigns on revenue generation.
- Attribution Modeling: Determine how different marketing touchpoints contribute to revenue and make data-driven decisions based on attribution modeling.

- Continuous Optimization: Regularly analyze campaign data and insights to refine your ABM approach. Adapt your strategy based on what's working and what needs adjustment.
- Reporting and Feedback Loop: Generate reports that provide a clear view of the ROI and success of your ABM campaigns. Use these reports to inform future decisions and refine your ABM strategy.

V. Alignment and Collaboration

- Sales and Marketing Alignment: Foster strong alignment and collaboration between sales and marketing teams to ensure that efforts are coordinated and targeted.
- Customer Success Integration: Involve customer success teams in the ABM strategy to ensure that customer retention and satisfaction are integral parts of the plan.
- Feedback and Communication: Establish regular communication channels to gather feedback from sales and customer success teams and adjust the ABM strategy accordingly.

VI. Scaling and Growth

- Scaling Up: Once you've established the effectiveness of your ABM strategy, consider expanding it to target more high-value accounts and additional segments.
- Continuous Learning: Encourage a culture of continuous learning and adaptability within your organization to stay updated with industry trends and evolving customer needs.

Remember that your ABM framework should be a flexible guide that can adapt to changing market conditions and account dynamics. Regularly assess the performance of your ABM campaigns and be prepared to refine and evolve your strategy to maximize its effectiveness.

CHAPTER 2

PRECISE TARGETING AND FOCUS IN B2B ACCOUNT-BASED MARKETING (ABM)

Now, it's time to discuss precise targeting and focus, which are fundamental elements of successful B2B Account-Based Marketing (ABM). ABM is a strategy that involves identifying and engaging specific high-value accounts rather than casting a wide net to reach a broad audience. Precise targeting ensures that your resources, efforts, and messaging are concentrated on accounts that are most likely to convert, resulting in a higher return on investment (ROI). Let's look at what precise targeting and focus entail, how to implement them in B2B ABM, and the key steps to create an effective ABM campaign.

What Is Precise Targeting and Focus in B2B ABM

Precise targeting and focus in B2B ABM involve the strategic selection of key accounts that align with your business goals and ideal customer profiles. Rather than pursuing a mass marketing approach, where you target a broad audience based on demographics or industry, ABM narrows the focus to a select group of high-potential accounts. Begin by determining who are your potential customers. What industry, what revenue size, what titles and functional areas of the business are they responsible for in their organization. Are you targeting the finance department, operations, logistics, sales, or marketing? Who are the highest decision-makers that you need to target, a C-level executive, VP, or director? The core principle of precise targeting and focus on ABM is treating each target account as a market of one. Each of your targets will need targeted messaging specific to their functional responsibilities. You will need to communicate with use cases and business outcomes that are tailored to their job function and responsibilities.

Key Components of Precise Targeting and Focus:

- Account Selection: The process begins with the identification of high-value target accounts that represent the best potential customers. This selection is often a collaborative effort between the sales and marketing teams and is based on data and insights.
- Customized Content and Messaging: Once target accounts are identified, the marketing team creates highly personalized content and messaging that resonates with the specific needs, challenges, and pain points of each account. This ensures that the content is highly relevant and engaging.
- Account-Specific Strategies: Each target account may require a unique marketing strategy based on its industry, position in the sales funnel, and other variables. These strategies are designed to maximize the chances of conversion.
- Multichannel Approach: ABM employs a multichannel approach, utilizing various marketing channels such as

email, social media, webinars, and direct outreach to reach and engage the individuals within the target accounts.

- Alignment with Sales: Precise targeting and focus require close collaboration between the sales and marketing teams. Sales and marketing collaborate to ensure that the messaging and outreach are coordinated and that the efforts are mutually reinforcing.
- Measurement and Analysis: Precise targeting and focus rely on detailed measurement and analysis to evaluate the effectiveness of campaigns and make data-driven adjustments. Metrics often include engagement rates, conversion rates, and the impact on revenue.

Now, let's explore how to implement precise targeting and focus in B2B ABM.

Implementing Precise Targeting and Focus in B2B ABM

Implementing precise targeting and focus in B2B ABM involves a structured approach that combines data-driven insights, strategic planning, and effective execution. Here are the key steps to implement precise targeting and focus in B2B ABM:

Define Your Ideal Customer Profile (ICP)

Before you can begin identifying target accounts, you must have a clear understanding of your ideal customer profile. Your ICP outlines the characteristics of the accounts that are the best fit for your products or services. Consider factors such as industry, company size, location, revenue, pain points, and challenges. This profile serves as the foundation for selecting target accounts.

Collaborate with Sales

ABM is most effective when marketing and sales teams work in close collaboration. Marketing should not operate in isolation when selecting target accounts. Instead, it should involve sales representatives in the decision-making process. Sales can provide valuable insights into the accounts that have the greatest potential and are currently in the sales pipeline.

Identify Target Accounts

Once you have a well-defined ICP and have consulted with your sales team, it's time to identify your target accounts. Start by leveraging your CRM data, market research, and third-party data sources to create a list of accounts that match your ICP criteria. These accounts should represent the highest revenue potential and strategic value for your business.

Prioritize Target Accounts

Not all target accounts are equal. Some may have a higher potential for immediate conversion, while others may be part of a longer-term strategy. Prioritize your target accounts based on their readiness to engage and buy. Consider factors like the level of engagement they've shown with your brand and their position in the buying journey.

Develop Account-Specific Strategies

With your target accounts selected and prioritized, it's time to create account-specific strategies. Each target account may require a unique approach based on factors such as their industry, challenges, and pain points. Tailor your content, messaging, and outreach to align with the specific needs of each account. Your goal is to demonstrate a deep understanding of their business and provide solutions that resonate.

Create Highly Personalized Content

Content is a cornerstone of ABM. Develop content that speaks directly to the challenges and goals of each target account. This may include whitepapers, case studies, industry-specific reports, and personalized messages from your team. Personalization is critical to engaging and resonating with decision-makers at the account.

Execute Multichannel Campaigns

ABM is not limited to a single channel. Implement multichannel campaigns to reach decision-makers within the target accounts. This may include email marketing, social media advertising, webinars, direct mail, and personalized one-on-one outreach. The choice of channels should align with the preferences of your target accounts.

Align Sales and Marketing Efforts

To ensure a cohesive and practical approach, maintain strong alignment between sales and marketing efforts. Communication is crucial, with both teams sharing insights, updates, and feedback regularly. Marketing should equip sales with the tools and information needed to engage with target accounts effectively.

Measure and Analyze Results

Implement a robust measurement and analysis framework to assess the performance of your ABM campaigns. Track metrics such as engagement rates, conversion rates, revenue impact, and the return on investment (ROI). Use this data to make data-driven adjustments and optimize your strategies.

Continuously Refine Strategies

ABM is an iterative process. As you gain more insights into the preferences and behaviors of your target accounts, continuously refine your strategies. Adapt your approach based on what works and what doesn't. Successful ABM requires a commitment to ongoing improvement.

This may seem like a lot of work and effort. Still, the benefits of precise targeting and focus mean that you are going to generate qualified leads for your organization and engage accounts that are ready to purchase your solutions.

Let's remind ourselves of the key benefits:

- Higher Conversion Rates: By concentrating your efforts on high-potential accounts, you're more likely to see higher conversion rates, resulting in increased revenue.
- Improved Customer Relationships: Personalized, targeted outreach fosters stronger relationships with target accounts. It demonstrates a deep understanding of their needs and challenges.
- Enhanced ROI: Precise targeting reduces resource wastage, leading to a better return on investment for your marketing efforts.
- Better Alignment with Sales: Collaboration between sales and marketing ensures a more coordinated and effective approach to engaging target accounts.

- Data-Driven Decision-Making: The analysis of ABM campaigns provides valuable insights for data-driven decision-making, allowing for continuous improvement.
- Competitive Advantage: ABM allows you to stand out in the eyes of your competition and your marketplace.

CHAPTER 3

PERSONALIZED CONTENT AND RELEVANCE MESSAGING

In the world of B2B marketing, the power of personalization and relevance cannot be overstated. Today's business buyers expect highly tailored and pertinent content that directly addresses their specific challenges and needs. To build creditability, your marketing content needs to articulate the proposed use case and utilize industry terms within your messaging that resonate with the audience. This level of personalization provides proof that you understand their needs and that you are knowledgeable of industry terminology. This is where Account-Based Marketing (ABM) comes into play, allowing marketers to create a one-to-one connection with target accounts. In this section, we'll explore the significance of personalization and relevance in a B2B ABM program, the techniques and strategies to implement them effectively, and the key benefits they bring to the table.

The Significance of Personalization and Relevance in B2B ABM

In B2B marketing, personalization and relevance are central to creating engaging and effective campaigns. Rather than employing a one-size-fits-all approach, ABM emphasizes crafting content and messages that speak directly to the unique needs and challenges of individual target accounts. This strategy ensures that your efforts resonate with decision-makers and influencers within those accounts, fostering deeper engagement and increasing the likelihood of conversion.

Key Elements of Personalization and Relevance in B2B ABM:

- **Account-Centric Approach:** ABM is inherently account-centric. It involves treating each target account as a market of one and tailoring your efforts to match their specific requirements. This approach is the foundation for personalization and relevance.

- **Highly Targeted Content:** Personalization begins with creating content that directly addresses the pain points, goals, and industry-specific challenges of your target accounts. This content should be precise and relatable to each account's unique context.

- **Segmentation and Buyer Personas:** Understanding the roles and personas within your target accounts is critical. By segmenting your audience and aligning your messaging with these personas, you can deliver more relevant content that speaks directly to their responsibilities and concerns.

- **Customized Messaging:** Tailor you're messaging to each account's particular needs. This means using language and examples that resonate with the account's industry, challenges, and goals. The messaging should reflect a deep understanding of the account's situation.

- **Multi-Channel Engagement:** Personalization and relevance should be applied across multiple marketing channels, from email and social media to webinars and direct outreach. This multichannel approach ensures that your message is consistently tailored.

Benefits of Personalization and Relevance in B2B ABM:

- **Higher Engagement:** Personalized content is more engaging, as it directly addresses the account's specific needs and challenges. Decision-makers are more likely to pay attention and interact with content that is relevant to them.
- **Improved Conversion Rates:** The relevance of your content and messaging increases the chances of conversion. When your messaging resonates with the account's concerns, they are more likely to take action, whether it's requesting more information or making a purchase.
- **Enhanced Customer Relationships:** By demonstrating a deep understanding of the account's needs and providing solutions, personalization fosters stronger customer relationships. This trust and credibility are crucial in the B2B sales process.
- **Reduced Wastage:** Personalization reduces wastage by ensuring that your marketing resources are spent on efforts that are more likely to convert. You're not sending generic messages to accounts that aren't a good fit for your offering.
- **Brand Differentiation:** In a competitive B2B landscape, personalization sets you apart from competitors. It positions your brand as one that genuinely understands and caters to the unique needs of your target accounts.

Now, let's explore how to implement personalization and relevance in a B2B ABM program effectively.

Personalization and relevance in B2B ABM require a structured approach that involves data analysis, content creation, and effective execution. Here are the key steps to implement personalization and relevance in a B2B ABM program:

1. Understand Your Target Accounts

To personalize effectively, you need to have a deep understanding of your target accounts. This includes knowledge of their industry, challenges, goals, and pain points. Leverage data from your CRM, market research, and interactions with the account to build a comprehensive profile.

2. Segment Your Audience

Not all individuals within an account have the same responsibilities and concerns. Segment your audience based on their roles and personas within the account. Understand the needs and priorities of each segment, as this will inform your content and messaging.

3. Create Account-Specific Content

Develop content that speaks directly to the challenges and goals of each target account. This may include whitepapers, case studies, industry-specific reports, and personalized messages from your team. The content should be particular and relatable to the account's unique context.

4. Tailor Messaging

Craft messaging that is specific to the account's needs and industry. This may involve using industry-specific terminology, providing examples that resonate with their challenges, and using language that reflects a deep understanding of their situation.

5. Leverage Automation and Personalization Tools

Use marketing automation and personalization tools to streamline the personalization process. These tools can help you create dynamic content that adapts to the account's characteristics, making it easier to personalize at scale.

6. Multichannel Engagement

Apply personalization and relevance across multiple marketing channels. This includes email marketing, social media advertising, webinars, direct mail, and personalized one-on-one outreach. Ensure that the messaging is consistently tailored and relevant across these channels.

7. Monitor and Adjust

Track the performance of your personalized campaigns. Pay attention to engagement metrics, conversion rates, and the impact on revenue. Use this data to adjust your strategies, ensuring that they remain relevant and practical.

Benefits of Personalization and Relevance

You will continue to read throughout this book the importance of creating and executing highly personalized content and messaging. Your campaigns will be more successful. You will see a higher level of engagement across all your campaigns; specific benefits include:

- **Higher Engagement:** Personalized content and messaging are more likely to capture the attention of your target accounts, resulting in higher engagement rates.
- **Improved Conversion Rates:** The relevance of your content increases the likelihood of conversion. Decision-makers are more inclined to take action when they find the content resonates with their specific challenges and needs.
- **Enhanced Customer Relationships:** By demonstrating a deep understanding of the account's needs and providing solutions, personalization fosters stronger customer relationships. Trust and credibility are pivotal in B2B relationships.
- **Reduced Resource Wastage:** Personalization ensures that your marketing resources are spent on efforts that are more likely to convert. You avoid sending generic messages to accounts that are not a good fit for your offering.
- **Brand Differentiation:** In a competitive B2B landscape, personalization sets your brand apart. It positions your brand as one that genuinely understands and caters to the unique needs of your target accounts.
- **Increased Customer Loyalty:** Effective personalization and relevance in ABM can lead to higher customer loyalty. When your targeted accounts see that you understand their specific challenges and consistently

provide valuable solutions, they are more likely to continue doing business with you.
- **Word-of-Mouth Referrals:** Satisfied, engaged accounts are more likely to recommend your brand to others in their network. Word-of-mouth referrals can lead to new business opportunities and growth.
- **Data-Driven Decision-Making:** The data collected from your ABM campaigns provides valuable insights for data-driven decision-making. You can continuously refine your strategies based on what works and what is not working. Such as which lead profile is conversing consistently, how many touches it requires, how it is improving the sales process, and the overall timing from lead conversion to close won proposals.

CHAPTER 4

DIGITAL ADVERTISING AND ACCOUNT-BASED MARKETING

Managing Digital Advertising in Account-Based Marketing (ABM) requires a strategic approach that aligns with the specific goals of your business. Who are you trying to reach, which website do they visit, and which publication, or online media and social media site do they typically visit for their industry content and insights? Do they subscribe to industry email newsletters, or listen to specific podcasts? In other words, who is their trusted source for their preferred content? You want to run your advertising across media outlets that your target market already trusts and consumes.

Next, consider the type of content that you need to promote and distribute in digital advertising that shows thought leadership, presents business challenges, and informs how to derive outcomes. Start thinking about the messages that you want to promote and how they will complement your brand value.

ABM is a targeted marketing strategy that focuses on high-value accounts or prospects, treating them as individual markets. The goal is to build personalized relationships and drive engagement with key decision-makers within those accounts. For example, your content should not be about your product or solution. Instead, it should be how your product and solution solve a business problem. In the digital advertising realm, this involves tailoring your online campaigns to resonate with the needs and interests of the specific accounts. In this comprehensive guide, we will delve into the key aspects of managing digital advertising in ABM and provide five practical examples to illustrate these concepts.

Managing Digital Advertising in Account-Based Marketing

Now, let's explore the steps involved in researching, creating, executing, and managing digital advertising within an ABM framework:

Define Advertising Objectives

Clearly define your advertising objectives within the context of ABM. Are you aiming to increase brand awareness, drive website traffic, or generate leads within specific target accounts? Understanding your objectives will guide the development of your digital advertising strategy.

Select the Right Advertising Channels

Identify the most effective digital advertising channels to reach your target accounts. This could include:

Social Media Advertising: Platforms like LinkedIn, Twitter, and Facebook allow for highly targeted advertising based on job titles, company size, and other relevant criteria. For example, "Is your audience on Linkedin or Facebook?" The answer is that most people are on both platforms. But how they consume and participate on these platforms is different. So, keep that in mind.

Display Advertising: Use display ads on relevant industry websites or through programmatic advertising to reach your target audience. Don't run your ads across the entire site. Be selective on your target audience, target only people who work for a certain organization or have a specific title that you are aiming or looking for. Better targeting will lead to qualified leads and less cost per lead.

Search Engine Advertising: Leverage "Pay-per-Click (PPC)" campaigns on search engines to ensure your brand appears when key decision-makers are searching for relevant solutions. And consider display network advertising with "Search Engine Marketing." But implement a retargeting display advertising so that your display ads are only shown to people who have already expressed interest in your brand or solution.

Develop Personalized Ad Content: Craft ad content that speaks directly about the pain points and goals of the individuals within the target accounts. This could involve creating different ad creatives for different personas within the same account.

Utilize Account-Based Targeting: In ABM, account-based targeting is crucial. Instead of targeting broad audience segments, narrow down your focus to the specific accounts and decision-makers you want to reach. Use account-based targeting options provided by advertising platforms to ensure your ads are seen by the right people.

Implement Retargeting Strategies: Implement retargeting strategies to stay "top-of-mind" with individuals from target accounts who have interacted with your digital ads or visited your website. This involves displaying follow-up ads to individuals who have shown interest but may not have converted.

Measure and Analyze Performance: Regularly monitor the performance of your digital advertising campaigns. Track key metrics such as click-through rates, conversion rates, and engagement specific to your target accounts. Use this data to refine and optimize your campaigns over time.

Integration with Marketing Automation: Integrate your digital advertising efforts with "Marketing Automation" tools. This ensures a seamless flow of data between your advertising platforms and other marketing systems, allowing for better targeting and personalization.

Dynamic Content Personalization: Consider using dynamic content personalization in your digital ads. This involves dynamically changing the content of your ads based on the characteristics and behavior of the viewer. For example, you can display different messages to individuals from different industries or show personalized greetings based on the viewer's role.

Here are five examples of digital advertising in the ABM model that you review to give you ideas on how you can build this for your campaigns. Now, let's explore five practical examples of how digital advertising can be effectively managed within an ABM framework:

Example 1: LinkedIn Sponsored Content for Enterprise Software

Objective: Increase awareness and consideration for a B2B enterprise software solution within specific Fortune 500 companies.

Strategy: Utilize LinkedIn Sponsored Content to target decision-makers in IT and C-level executives within the identified Fortune 500 companies. Craft personalized ad copy highlighting how the software addresses the specific challenges faced by large enterprises.

Use LinkedIn's **account targeting feature** to ensure that the ads are seen by individuals from the targeted companies.

Measurement: Monitors click-through rates (CTR) and engagement metrics for the targeted companies. Track the number of leads generated from the targeted accounts.

Example 2: Programmatic Display Ads for Financial Services

Objective: Generate leads for a financial services company targeting mid-sized businesses in the finance sector.

Strategy: Implement "Programmatic Display Advertising" on industry-specific websites and financial news platforms.

Develop visually engaging display ads with personalized messaging for finance professionals. Utilize programmatic targeting options to focus on companies within the desired size range.

Measurement: Track lead generation metrics from companies within the finance sector. Analyze the conversion rates for the targeted audience.

Example 3: Google Ads for SaaS Solution

Objective: Increase product trials for a SaaS solution targeting small and medium-sized businesses (SMBs).

Strategy: Implement "Google Ads campaigns" targeting keywords relevant to SMB software needs.

Create ad copy that emphasizes the ease of use and specific benefits for SMBs. Utilize Google Ads audience targeting options to focus on businesses within the defined size range.

Measurement: Monitor the number of product trial sign-ups from SMBs. Analyze the click-through rates and conversion rates for the targeted audience.

Example 4: Twitter Promoted Tweets for Marketing Agency

Objective: Drive engagement with a marketing agency's content and attract potential clients from specific industries.

Strategy: Use "Twitter Promoted Tweets" to amplify the agency's thought leadership content. Tailor ad content to address the marketing challenges faced by companies in target industries. Leverage Twitter's targeting options to reach decision-makers within the identified industries.

Measurement: Track engagement metrics such as likes, retweets, and clicks on the agency's promoted tweets. Monitor website traffic from Twitter to assess the impact on lead generation.

Example 5: Facebook Carousel Ads for E-commerce

Objective: Increase sales for an e-commerce company targeting individual consumers.

Strategy: Implement Facebook Carousel Ads showcasing a variety of products tailored to different customer segments. Use Facebook's audience targeting options to focus on demographics, interests, and online behavior. Include personalized offers and incentives in the ad copy to drive conversions.

Measurement: Track e-commerce sales attributed to the Facebook Carousel Ads. Analyze engagement metrics such as clicks and interactions with specific products.

Effectively managing digital advertising in ABM requires a strategic and personalized approach. By understanding the core principles of ABM and implementing targeted digital advertising strategies, businesses can build meaningful relationships with key accounts and drive measurable results. The examples provided above demonstrate how different advertising channels and strategies can be tailored to specific objectives within an ABM framework. As the digital landscape continues to evolve, staying abreast of emerging technologies and trends will be essential for maximizing the impact of digital advertising in the context of account-based marketing.

CHAPTER 5

UNDERSTANDING THE ROLE OF SOCIAL MEDIA IN ACCOUNT-BASED MARKETING

Social media is an integral part of modern marketing strategies and its role is particularly significant in the realm of Account-Based Marketing (ABM). Social media is where we all go to connect with colleagues and friends. It's where we get our news these days. It's where we find out what other people are doing, which industry events they are attending, who is speaking at the events, or what new product or initiative was launched by our partners or competitors.

Remember, ABM is a strategic approach that tailors marketing efforts to specific high-value accounts, treating them as individual markets. In this chapter, we will explore how to effectively use social media for Account-Based Marketing, covering key strategies and best practices and providing practical examples.

1. Identifying Target Accounts: In ABM, the first crucial step is to identify and prioritize target accounts. Social media platforms provide a wealth of information that can be utilized for this purpose. By leveraging features like LinkedIn's "Company

Pages" you can gain insights into the structure, size, and recent activities of potential target accounts.

Example: Company XYZ, a B2B software provider, has decided to focus on enterprise-level accounts in the finance sector. Using LinkedIn, they identify key decision-makers, recent hires, and ongoing projects within their target accounts.

2. Building Relationships and Understanding Interests: Social media is a powerful tool for building relationships with key stakeholders within target accounts. Following, connecting, and engaging with individuals on platforms like LinkedIn and Twitter can provide valuable insights into their professional interests, challenges, and the content they find relevant.

Example: The marketing team at Company XYZ engages with the LinkedIn posts and Twitter updates of key contacts within target accounts. They share relevant industry insights, comment on posts, and participate in discussions to build rapport and gain a deeper understanding of the challenges faced by these accounts.

Let's go ahead and begin to develop a social media strategy for ABM. One question should be, "Which platform(s) should be our choice for our marketing campaign?"

1. Platform Selection: Not all social media platforms are created equal and the choice of platforms should align with the preferences and habits of your target audience. LinkedIn is often a primary platform for B2B interactions, given its professional nature, but other platforms like Twitter and even industry-specific forums can also play a crucial role.

Example: Company XYZ, after researching their target accounts, finds that decision-makers in the finance sector are actively engaged on LinkedIn. They decided to focus their primary efforts on LinkedIn for direct interactions and industry forums for more specialized discussions.

2. Content Creation and Distribution: Crafting and sharing relevant content is key to capturing the attention of target accounts on social media. This includes a mix of thought leadership articles, case studies, infographics, and other content types that resonate with the challenges and interests of your target audience.

Example: To showcase their expertise, Company XYZ creates a series of LinkedIn articles addressing common challenges in the finance sector, such as cybersecurity concerns. They also share success stories and case studies highlighting how their software has helped similar organizations overcome these challenges.

3. Personalized Messaging: ABM thrives on personalized communication and social media provides an opportunity for direct and tailored messaging. Whether through private messages or public comments, ensure that your interactions are personalized and relevant to the specific needs of each target account.

Example: When reaching out to a key decision-maker in a target account, the sales team at Company XYZ references recent posts or articles shared by that individual. They highlight specific features of their software that align with the challenges mentioned in the target contact's recent posts.

4. Social Listening: "Social Listening" involves monitoring social media channels for mentions of your brand, competitors, and industry keywords. In the context of ABM, social listening can provide real-time insights into the discussions and concerns of your target accounts.

Example: Using social listening tools, Company XYZ monitors social media for discussions related to finance software. When a key account mentions challenges with their current software provider, Company XYZ can proactively reach out with a personalized solution.

5. Paid Social Advertising: Social media platforms offer robust advertising options, allowing you to target specific accounts or individuals based on their profile information. Invest in paid social advertising to ensure your content reaches the right people within your target accounts.

Example: Company XYZ uses LinkedIn's targeted advertising to reach decision-makers in their identified target accounts. They create sponsored content highlighting the "Unique Value Proposition" of their software and ensure it appears in the feeds of key stakeholders within the finance sector.

Now that you have built your social media program, it's time to Integrate social media within the overall ABM Strategy.

1. Alignment with Sales Teams: For successful ABM, alignment between marketing and sales teams is crucial. Social media interactions should seamlessly integrate with overall sales efforts, ensuring a consistent and coordinated approach.

Example: The marketing and sales teams at Company XYZ hold regular meetings to discuss ongoing social media interactions. The sales team provides insights into the specific challenges faced by target accounts, enabling the marketing team to tailor their social media content accordingly.

2. Data Integration: Integrate social media data with your Customer Relationship Management (CRM) system to create a comprehensive view of interactions with target accounts. This integration ensures that both marketing and sales teams have access to the latest information when engaging with accounts.

Example: Company XYZ uses a CRM system that integrates seamlessly with social media platforms. When a sales representative engages with a contact on LinkedIn, this interaction is automatically logged in the CRM, providing a unified view of the account's history and activities.

3. Metrics and Analytics: Define key performance indicators (KPIs) for your social media efforts in ABM. Track metrics such as engagement rates, click-through rates, and the number of interactions with target accounts to assess the effectiveness of your social media strategy.

Example: Company XYZ sets KPIs for their LinkedIn campaign, aiming to achieve a 20% increase in engagement rates and a 15% growth in the number of connections within their target accounts. Regular analytics reviews help them adjust their strategy for optimal results.

The world of social media and digital marketing today comes with both, overcoming challenges and maximizing opportunities. Below are some things that you should be aware of.

1. Privacy and Compliance: Ensure that your social media activities adhere to privacy regulations and platform policies. Obtain consent where necessary and respect the boundaries of your target accounts.

Example: Company XYZ, aware of privacy concerns, includes a disclaimer in their LinkedIn connection requests, clearly stating the purpose of the connection and providing options for individuals to opt out of further communications.

2. Content Relevance: Maintain a keen focus on the relevance of your content. In the fast-paced world of social media, irrelevant or generic content can quickly be dismissed.

Example: To address this challenge, Company XYZ regularly surveys its target accounts to understand evolving challenges and interests. They use this feedback to adjust their content strategy, ensuring that their social media content remains highly relevant.

3. Continuous Monitoring and Adaptation: Social media landscapes evolve, and it's crucial to stay abreast of changes in algorithms, user behaviors, and industry trends. Regularly monitor your social media strategy and adapt to emerging opportunities.

Example: Company XYZ invests in ongoing training for their social media team to stay updated on the latest features of platforms like LinkedIn. They also participate in industry webinars and forums to gain insights into evolving trends in B2B social media marketing.

Leveraging social media for Account-Based Marketing requires a strategic approach. By identifying target accounts, building relationships, and crafting a personalized and relevant social media strategy, businesses can enhance their ABM efforts and increase the likelihood of engagement with high-value accounts in real-time.

CHAPTER 6

PROMOTING EVENTS WITH ACCOUNT-BASED MARKETING

In the dynamic landscape of B2B marketing, events, conferences, and tradeshows remain powerful tools for engagement, networking, and brand exposure. Account-Based Marketing (ABM), a strategic approach that targets specific high-value accounts, can be a game-changer when it comes to promoting events. This guide will delve into the intricacies of leveraging ABM to promote events effectively, covering key strategies and best practices, and providing practical examples.

Understanding the Role of ABM in Event Promotion

1. Identifying Target Accounts for Events: Before diving into event promotion, it's crucial to identify and prioritize the target accounts that align with the goals of the event. ABM emphasizes a personalized approach, treating each account as a market of its own. Start by leveraging data and insights to pinpoint accounts with the highest potential value for your event.

Example: Company XYZ, a B2B software provider, is hosting a technology conference. Using ABM principles, they identify key accounts within the finance and healthcare sectors as potential attendees, focusing on decision-makers who align with the event's theme.

2. Creating Personalized Invitations: ABM thrives on personalization, and event invitations are no exception. Craft tailored invitations that speak directly to the interests and pain points of your target accounts. Consider using personalized videos, custom landing pages, or interactive elements to make your invitation stand out.

Example: Company XYZ creates personalized event invitations for each target account, highlighting specific sessions, speakers, or networking opportunities that would be particularly relevant to that account's industry or challenges.

1. Account-Centric Content Marketing: Tailor your content marketing efforts to align with the interests and needs of your target accounts. Develop blog posts, articles, and other content pieces that showcase the value of attending your event and address the specific concerns of your target audience.

Example: Leading up to the event, Company XYZ publishes a series of blog posts on topics related to the challenges faced by their target accounts. These posts serve as teasers for the event content and encourage engagement from the identified accounts.

2. Multi-Channel Engagement: Utilize a multi-channel approach to engage with your target accounts across various platforms. This includes email campaigns, social media interactions, and even direct outreach through channels like LinkedIn. Consistent and coordinated engagement enhances the visibility of your event.

Example: Company XYZ launches a multi-channel engagement campaign, starting with personalized email invitations. They follow up with targeted social media posts on LinkedIn and Twitter, engaging with key contacts within the target accounts and fostering excitement about the upcoming event.

3. Personalized Event Website Experience: Create a personalized experience for target accounts when they visit your event website. Use dynamic content that caters to the interests of each account, showcasing relevant sessions, speakers, and networking opportunities. Implement personalized landing pages for specific accounts.

Example: When contacts from target accounts visit the event website, Company XYZ's website dynamically adjusts to showcase content that aligns with the industry and challenges of that account. Personalized landing pages provide a seamless and tailored experience.

4. Account-Specific Webinars and Pre-Event Content: Host webinars or create pre-event content specifically designed for your target accounts. This not only builds anticipation for the event but also positions your brand as a valuable resource, catering to the unique needs of each account.

Example: Company XYZ organizes a series of pre-event webinars, each addressing a specific challenge faced by their target accounts. These webinars serve as a precursor to the event, providing valuable insights and generating interest among the identified accounts.

5. ABM with Influencers and Thought Leaders: Leverage influencers and thought leaders in your industry to amplify your event promotion efforts. Identify influencers relevant to your target accounts and collaborate with them to create content, host webinars, or participate in promotional activities.

Example: Company XYZ partners with industry influencers who have a significant following within their target accounts. These influencers share personalized messages about the event, vouching for its relevance and creating a buzz among their audience.

Integrating ABM with Event Logistics

1. **Personalized Event Swag and Collateral:** Extend personalization to the physical realm by creating personalized event swag and collateral. Send customized event packages to key contacts within target accounts, including branded items, relevant content, and personalized notes.

Example: In preparation for the event, Company XYZ sends personalized event packages to decision-makers within target accounts. These packages include branded merchandise, exclusive event content, and a personalized letter highlighting the value of their attendance.

2. **VIP Treatment for Target Accounts:** Offer VIP treatment to key contacts within target accounts. Provide exclusive access to certain sessions, networking opportunities, or even personalized one-on-one meetings with speakers. Make your target accounts feel valued and appreciated.

Example: During the event, Company XYZ designates a VIP lounge for key contacts within target accounts. They offer exclusive access to speakers, roundtable discussions, and networking events, providing a unique and memorable experience for these accounts.

3. Real-Time Engagement and Feedback: Encourage real-time engagement and feedback from target accounts during the event. Use event-specific hashtags, live polls, and interactive sessions to facilitate participation. Monitor social media and event platforms for insights and adjust your strategy accordingly.

Example: Company XYZ creates a dedicated event hashtag and encourages attendees from target accounts to share their experiences on social media. They actively monitor the hashtag, engage with posts, and use real-time feedback to enhance the event experience for participants.

Measuring Success and Adjusting Strategies

1. Define Key Metrics: Establish Key Performance Indicators (KPIs) to measure the success of your ABM-driven event promotion. Metrics may include the number of registrations from target accounts, engagement rates, and post-event surveys to gauge satisfaction.

Example: Company XYZ sets KPIs such as a 20% increase in registrations from target accounts compared to previous events and a minimum engagement rate of 15% on pre-event content. These metrics serve as benchmarks for success.

2. Post-Event Follow-Up: After the event, continue your personalized approach with post-event follow-ups. Send personalized thank-you emails, share event highlights, and request feedback from attendees within target accounts. Use post-event engagement to nurture ongoing relationships.

Example: Company XYZ sends personalized thank-you emails to attendees from target accounts, expressing gratitude for their participation. They include a summary of key event takeaways, exclusive content, and a request for feedback to inform future engagement.

3. Data Analysis and Iteration: Analyze the data collected during and after the event to derive actionable insights. Understand which strategies were most effective in engaging target accounts and iterate on your approach for future events.

Example: By analyzing post-event data, Company XYZ discovered that personalized webinars were particularly effective in driving registrations from target accounts. They decided to expand this strategy for future events and explore new ways to enhance personalization.

Challenges and Considerations in ABM Event Promotion

As you manage your marketing programs to support events, you will encounter challenges. This is normal. Some of your assumptions about the campaigns will be challenged. The key is to have good metrics in place to help you monitor the effectiveness of the programs and your ability to continuously pivot until you get the results that you want.

1. Data Accuracy and Integration: Maintaining accurate and integrated data is crucial for successful ABM event promotion. Ensure that data from various sources, including CRM systems and social media platforms, is up-to-date and seamlessly integrated.

Example: Company XYZ conducts regular data audits to ensure the accuracy of contact information within its CRM system. They also use automation tools to synchronize data between the CRM and social media platforms, creating a centralized and reliable source of information.

2. Personalization at Scale: Scaling personalization can be challenging, especially when dealing with a large number of target accounts. Invest in technologies that enable automated personalization and dynamic content delivery.

Example: To address the challenge of personalization at scale, Company XYZ employs marketing automation tools that allow them to create dynamic content based on account-specific data. This enables them to deliver personalized experiences to a larger audience.

3. Privacy and Consent: Respect privacy regulations and obtain explicit consent for personalized interactions. Clearly communicate the purpose of data collection and use and provide opt-out options for individuals who do not wish to participate.

Example: Company XYZ includes a consent statement in their event registration process, clearly outlining how participant data will be used for personalized interactions. They provide options for attendees to customize their preferences and opt out of certain communications.

Effectively promoting events with Account-Based Marketing requires a strategic and personalized approach throughout the entire event lifecycle. From identifying target accounts to crafting personalized invitations, creating account-centric content, and offering VIP experiences during the event, ABM can significantly enhance the success of your events. By integrating social media, personalized content, and data-driven insights, businesses can not only drive attendance but also nurture valuable relationships with high-value accounts. Continuous analysis, iteration, and a commitment to privacy and consent will ensure the long-term success of your ABM-driven event promotion efforts in the ever-evolving landscape of B2B marketing.

CHAPTER 7

HOW TO IMPLEMENT WEBINARS AND PODCASTS TO ACCOUNT-BASED MARKETING

In this chapter, we are going to discuss how to implement Webinars and Podcasts within an Account-Based Marketing (ABM) strategy. Both webinars and podcasts offer opportunities to deliver high-quality content, establish thought leadership, and foster relationships with key decision-makers within specific target accounts. You may choose to have an account-specific webinar and podcast or execute broad messaging and attract multiple accounts at the same time. Let's explore the steps to effectively integrate webinars and podcasts into an ABM approach, along with five detailed examples.

Integrating Webinars in Account-Based Marketing

1. Identify Target Accounts and Topics

- **Objective:** Determine the key accounts you aim to engage with and understand their pain points and challenges.
- **Strategy:** Select webinar topics that directly address the needs of these accounts. For instance, if targeting

healthcare organizations, a webinar on "Transforming Patient Care through Technology" could be relevant.

2. Personalize Invitations and Content

- **Objective:** Tailor invitations and content to resonate with each target account.
- **Strategy:** Customize invitations by mentioning specific challenges or opportunities the account faces. Additionally, personalize the webinar content by referencing the account's industry or specific pain points within the presentation.

3. Host Exclusive Webinars for Target Accounts

- **Objective:** Provide an exclusive experience for targeted accounts.
- **Strategy:** Organize dedicated webinars exclusively for selected accounts or industries. For example, hosting a private session titled "Digital Solutions for Retail Giants" for key players in the retail sector.

4. Follow-up with Personalized Content

- **Objective:** Nurture relationships and continue engagement post-webinar.
- **Strategy:** Send follow-up emails with resources related to the webinar content, such as whitepapers, case studies, or additional insights specifically curated for the account's needs.

5. Measure Engagement and Impact

- **Objective:** Assess the effectiveness of the webinar in engaging target accounts.
- **Strategy:** Track metrics like attendee engagement, post-webinar interactions, and eventual conversions or interactions that result from the webinar's content.

Below are a few examples of Webinars in ABM

Example 1: Software Solutions for Financial Institutions

Objective: Engage with decision-makers in regional banks to showcase a software solution's benefits.

Strategy: Create a webinar titled "Future-Proofing Financial Institutions: Tech Solutions for Growth."

- Customize invitations mentioning challenges specific to regional banks.
- Offer post-webinar consultations tailored to each bank's needs.

Example 2: Healthcare Innovation for Hospitals

Objective: Position a healthcare tech company as an innovator in hospital technology.

Strategy: Host a webinar on "Revolutionizing Patient Care: AI-Powered Solutions for Hospitals."

- Personalize invitations with hospital-specific challenges.
- Provide case studies and success stories during the webinar.

How To Integrate Podcasts in Account-Based Marketing

1. Identify Target Accounts and Topics

- Objective: Understand the interests and challenges of target accounts.
- Strategy: Choose podcast topics that align with the industries or pain points of these accounts. For instance, an episode titled "Innovations in Retail Tech" for retail-focused accounts.

2. Feature Accounts in Podcast Episodes

- Objective: Showcase accounts as industry leaders.
- Strategy: Invite key decision-makers from target accounts as guest speakers to discuss industry trends or share insights in a podcast episode.

3. Create Tailored Content for Accounts

- Objective: Deliver content that resonates with specific accounts.
- Strategy: Develop episodes that delve into challenges faced by target accounts and provide solutions or expert insights tailored to their needs.

4. Promote Episodes Strategically

- Objective: Ensure episodes reach the intended audience within target accounts.
- Strategy: Share podcast episodes via targeted email campaigns or LinkedIn messages, ensuring they reach the right individuals within the accounts.

5. Measure Impact and Engagement

- Objective: Evaluate the effectiveness of podcast episodes in engaging target accounts.
- Strategy: Track downloads, listener engagement, and any subsequent interactions or inquiries from the target accounts post-episode.

Examples of Podcasts in ABM

Example 3: Technology Solutions for Manufacturing Giants

- Objective: Engage with decision-makers in the manufacturing sector to showcase technology solutions.
- Strategy: Produce a podcast episode titled "Smart Manufacturing: Transforming Operations with Technology."
- Feature interviews with industry experts discussing challenges faced by manufacturing giants.

Example 4: Financial Advisory for Corporate Clients

- Objective: Position a financial advisory firm as a thought leader in corporate finance.
- Strategy: Create episodes focusing on financial challenges for large corporations.
- Invite CFOs or financial executives from targeted companies as guests to share their insights.

Example 5: Legal Services for Tech Startups

- Objective: Engage with tech startups seeking legal counsel and services.

- Strategy: Develop podcast episodes covering legal challenges specific to tech startups.
- Interview startup founders or legal experts to provide insights and advice tailored to this audience.

By integrating webinars and podcasts into your ABM strategy, with personalized content and targeted engagement, you can create meaningful interactions that resonate with key decision-makers within your target accounts, nurturing stronger relationships and driving business growth.

CHAPTER 8

LEVERAGING ABM IN PUBLIC RELATIONS STRATEGIES

Account-Based Marketing (ABM) has evolved beyond traditional marketing strategies and has found applications in various domains including Public Relations (PR) and Thought Leadership. ABM, a highly targeted approach that focuses on personalized interactions with specific high-value accounts, aligns well with the goals of PR programs and Thought Leadership initiatives. Let's discuss how ABM principles can be applied effectively in PR and thought leadership content strategies. But first, let's understand the different components of PR and how Account-Based Marketing (ABM)approach can add value and apply to the following major components of PR:

Targeted Relationship Building: In PR, the emphasis is on building relationships with key stakeholders, journalists, influencers, and industry leaders.

ABM enables PR professionals to identify specific accounts (publications, journalists, influencers) and tailor communication and engagements to meet their unique preferences and needs. It's about nurturing personalized relationships rather than mass outreach.

Personalized Storytelling and Messaging: PR thrives on compelling storytelling and impactful messaging that resonates with the target audience.

ABM allows for tailored messaging and storytelling directed at specific accounts or individuals, addressing their pain points, interests, and industry-specific challenges. This personalized approach increases the likelihood of engagement and coverage.

Strategic Media Outreach: PR aims to secure media coverage and positive exposure for a brand or individual.

ABM strategies guide PR teams in identifying priority media outlets or journalists relevant to specific target accounts. This facilitates focused efforts on building relationships and crafting pitches that align with the interests of these outlets or journalists.

Building Thought Leadership: Establishing thought leadership involves positioning individuals or brands as industry experts.

ABM assists in identifying key accounts where thought leadership content can have the most impact. By tailoring content and engagements to these accounts, PR teams can amplify thought leadership efforts within specific niches or industries.

Identifying Target Accounts for Thought Leadership: Thought leadership aims to influence and educate specific audiences about industry trends, innovations, and best practices.

ABM principles help in identifying high-value accounts or decision-makers within industries or sectors where thought leadership content can make a significant impact. Content creation and distribution are then tailored to these accounts' interests and challenges.

Personalized Content Creation: Thought leadership content should be informative, valuable, and resonate with the audience.

ABM allows for the creation of personalized content addressing the specific pain points, interests, and challenges of target accounts or individuals. This customized approach increases engagement and credibility.

Focused Distribution and Amplification: Thought leadership content needs strategic dissemination to reach the right audience.

ABM enables targeted distribution channels and amplification efforts focused on reaching decision-makers within identified accounts. This could involve direct outreach, targeted social media campaigns, or partnerships with relevant industry platforms.

Building Relationships through Thought Leadership: Thought leadership content serves as a catalyst for building trust and credibility.

ABM strategies aid in fostering relationships by consistently delivering high-quality, insightful content to key accounts. This positions the brand or individual as a valuable resource, nurturing long-term relationships.

Measurement and Impact Assessment: Assessing the effectiveness of thought leadership efforts is crucial for refinement and optimization.

ABM allows for detailed measurement of thought leadership content performance within specific target accounts. Metrics such as engagement levels, content shares, or interactions with decision-makers help gauge impact and refine strategies.

Examples of ABM in PR Programs and Thought Leadership Content: Securing media coverage for a technology company's new product launch.

ABM Can Help With:

- Identifying key journalists or publications covering similar tech innovations.
- Tailoring personalized pitches, highlighting how the product addresses specific industry challenges.
- Engagement with these journalists through targeted interactions, offering exclusive insights or interviews.

Example of Thought Leadership Content: Establishing a CEO as an industry thought leader in sustainability.

ABM Can Help With:

- Identifying top sustainability-focused organizations or companies.
- Create content (articles, webinars, whitepapers) addressing sustainability challenges these organizations face.
- Distribute the content through personalized outreach and engage with decision-makers in these organizations.

ABM principles and tactics can be leveraged in PR programs and thought leadership content strategies enhance the effectiveness and impact of these initiatives. By building personalized relationships, tailored messaging, strategic outreach, and targeted content creation, PR professionals and thought leaders can effectively engage with high-value accounts, amplify brand visibility, and position themselves as industry authorities. ABM, when integrated with PR and thought leadership, drives meaningful engagements, fosters credibility, and cultivates lasting relationships with key stakeholders and decision-makers.

CHAPTER 9

STRONG SALES AND MARKETING ALIGNMENT IN B2B ACCOUNT-BASED MARKETING

In the realm of B2B marketing, one of the critical success factors for a thriving Account-Based Marketing (ABM) strategy is the alignment between sales and marketing teams. This alignment is not merely a *nice-to-have*; it's a necessity for effectively executing marketing campaigns. In this chapter, we'll explore the importance of stronger sales and marketing alignment in a B2B ABM approach, provide examples of successful alignment strategies, and discuss how this synergy can drive business growth.

The Importance of Sales and Marketing Alignment in B2B ABM

Sales and Marketing Alignment is crucial in the context of ABM because it ensures that both teams are working together cohesively to achieve shared goals. Here's why it's so important:

- **Unified Strategy:** ABM requires a unified strategy that identifies and targets high-value accounts. Sales and marketing alignment is essential in developing and executing this strategy.

- **Consistent Messaging:** When sales and marketing are aligned, it ensures that the messaging is consistent across all touchpoints. Prospects and clients receive the same messages and experience a seamless transition from marketing outreach to sales engagement.
- **Lead Nurturing:** ABM often involves a longer sales cycle with multiple touchpoints. Aligning sales and marketing teams ensures that leads are effectively nurtured, increasing the likelihood of conversion.
- **Account-Centric Approach:** ABM is inherently account-centric. Strong alignment between sales and marketing ensures that the focus is squarely on the accounts, rather than individual leads. This results in more effective and strategic outreach.
- **Feedback Loop:** Collaboration between sales and marketing teams facilitates the exchange of valuable feedback. Sales can provide insights into what's working or what messaging is resonating with accounts, helping marketing fine-tune their strategies.

Now, let's explore examples of how to achieve stronger sales and marketing alignment in a B2B ABM approach:

Example 1: Define and Prioritize Target Accounts Together

Sales and marketing alignment begins with the selection of target accounts. To ensure both teams are on the same page, they should collaboratively define and prioritize these accounts. For example, a marketing team might leverage data and analytics to identify high-value accounts based on industry, revenue potential, and fit with the ideal customer profile (ICP). Once the accounts are identified, sales and marketing teams should jointly assess their strategic value. This collaborative effort ensures that sales teams are enthusiastic about the chosen accounts and are committed to pursuing them actively.

Example Scenario: Imagine a software company that provides data analytics solutions for enterprise clients. The sales team and marketing team work together to identify a set of Fortune 500 companies as their target accounts. This alignment ensures that both teams are fully invested in pursuing these high-value accounts and have a shared understanding of their importance to the company's growth.

Example 2: Create a Shared Account Plan

A shared account plan is a detailed document that outlines the strategy and tactics for engaging a target account. It includes information about the account's challenges, goals, key decision-makers, and the specific actions both sales and marketing teams will take to move the account through the sales funnel. Creating a shared account plan facilitates alignment by providing a clear roadmap for how the two teams will work together to engage and convert the account.

Example Scenario: A cybersecurity company is targeting a large financial institution. The sales and marketing teams collaborate to create a shared account plan that includes personalized messaging, content, and a series of interactions. The plan also outlines the roles and responsibilities of each team. The shared account plan becomes a guide for the coordinated efforts of both sales and marketing teams.

Example 3: Regular Communication and Feedback

Open and regular communication between sales and marketing teams is essential for alignment. Meetings, joint discussions, and feedback sessions help the teams stay informed about the progress of ABM campaigns and share insights on what's working and what needs adjustment. Sales can provide feedback on the quality of leads generated by marketing efforts, while marketing can update sales on the performance of account-specific content and campaigns.

Example Scenario: In a Software-as-a-Service (SaaS) company, the sales and marketing teams meet every week to review the progress of ABM campaigns. The marketing team shares data on engagement rates and content performance, while the sales team provides insights on the quality of leads generated. This regular communication allows both teams to make data-driven decisions and fine-tune their strategies.

Benefits of Stronger Sales and Marketing Alignment in B2B ABM

The alignment of sales and marketing in a B2B ABM approach offers numerous benefits:

- **Higher Conversion Rates:** With a coordinated approach, both teams can work together to nurture leads and engage target accounts effectively, resulting in higher conversion rates.
- **Improved Customer Relationships:** The cohesive and consistent messaging fosters stronger customer relationships. When accounts experience a seamless

transition from marketing to sales, it builds trust and credibility.

- **Enhanced Customer Experience:** Aligning sales and marketing ensures that the entire customer experience, from the first touchpoint to the final sale, is consistent and aligned with the account's needs.
- **Streamlined Lead Nurturing:** Sales and marketing alignment streamlines the lead nurturing process. Leads are effectively passed from marketing to sales, ensuring that they receive the necessary attention at each stage of the sales funnel.
- **Data-Driven Decision-Making:** The collaboration between sales and marketing allows for the exchange of valuable feedback and insights. This data-driven approach helps both teams continuously refine their strategies.
- **Shorter Sales Cycles:** Strong alignment can lead to shorter sales cycles, as both teams work together to address the account's needs and move them through the funnel more efficiently.
- **Increased Revenue:** Ultimately, the alignment of sales and marketing contributes to increased revenue. When both teams are coordinated and working toward shared goals, the impact on the bottom line is substantial.

In summary, Sales and Marketing Alignment is a critical component of a successful B2B ABM approach. It ensures that both teams work together cohesively to engage and convert target accounts. By defining and prioritizing target accounts together, creating shared account plans, and maintaining regular communication, businesses can experience the benefits of higher conversion rates, improved customer relationships, and increased revenue. Strong alignment is not just a *nice-to-have*; it's a strategic imperative for businesses aiming to thrive in the competitive B2B landscape.

CHAPTER 10

HOW TO MANGE AND IMPROVED LEAD QUALITY

impacts the success of your campaigns. The term "lead quality" refers to the characteristics and attributes of leads that determine their potential to become valuable customers. It's not just about generating a high quantity of leads; it's about focusing on the right leads, those that are more likely to convert and contribute to your company's growth. In this comprehensive guide, we'll delve into what lead quality means in B2B ABM, why it's crucial, and provide examples to illustrate its importance.

What Is Lead Quality in B2B ABM: Lead quality in B2B ABM encompasses several key dimensions that collectively define the potential value of a lead. These dimensions often include:

- **Fit with Ideal Customer Profile (ICP):** A high-quality lead closely aligns with your ICP. This means that the lead's characteristics, such as industry, company size, and location, match the criteria that define your ideal customer.

- **Engagement and Interest:** Quality leads show an active interest in your products or services. They engage with your content, attend webinars, download resources, and may interact with your sales or marketing teams.
- **Decision-Making Authority:** Valuable leads often hold decision-making roles or influence the purchasing decisions within their organizations. These individuals can greenlight the purchase of your offerings.
- **Budget and Purchase Intent:** High-quality leads have the financial resources and the intent to invest in your solutions. They are more likely to have a budget allocated for the type of products or services you offer.
- **Relevance to ABM Strategy:** In ABM, lead quality extends beyond individual leads to the quality of the target account itself. Quality accounts align with your ABM strategy and represent high-value opportunities for your business.

Now, let's explore the importance of lead quality in B2B ABM with examples:

Efficiency in Resource Allocation: High lead quality allows your sales and marketing teams to allocate their resources more efficiently. Rather than pursuing leads that aren't a good fit or are unlikely to convert, your teams can focus their efforts on the leads that are more likely to bring value to your organization.

Example 1: A marketing team in a software company generates leads from a targeted campaign focused on specific industries and company sizes. By ensuring that these leads align with their ICP, the team can effectively allocate their resources to engage with them and convert them into customers.

Shorter Sales Cycles: Quality leads are often more informed and motivated to make purchasing decisions. This leads to shorter sales cycles, as your sales team doesn't have to spend excessive time educating leads or overcoming objections.

Example 2: A sales team in a cybersecurity firm receives a lead from a large enterprise that has actively shown interest in their solutions and fits their ICP. Due to the lead's high quality and readiness to invest in security measures, the sales cycle is significantly shorter, and the deal is closed faster.

Higher Conversion Rates: Lead quality directly correlates with conversion rates. When you focus on high-quality leads, you're more likely to see a higher percentage of these leads converting into customers. This not only maximizes your ROI but also boosts revenue.

Example 3: A marketing team running an ABM campaign for a financial software company targets leads from financial institutions. Since these leads closely match the ICP and have shown interest in financial software solutions, they achieve a higher conversion rate than broader, less-qualified leads.

Better Customer Lifetime Value: High-quality leads often have a higher customer lifetime value (CLV). This means they are not only more likely to convert but also to stay with your company, make repeat purchases, and potentially become advocates for your brand.

Example 4: A B2B marketing agency generates leads through an ABM campaign. The leads they attract are from businesses that closely match their ICP and are ready to invest in marketing services. Over time, these high-quality leads not only convert but also continue to engage with the agency, leading to a higher CLV.

Cost Savings: Pursuing high-quality leads can lead to cost savings. When you focus your marketing efforts on leads with a higher potential to convert, you reduce the expenses associated with generating and nurturing a large quantity of less-qualified leads.

Example 5: An industrial equipment manufacturer uses ABM to target leads from companies in specific industries and regions. By concentrating on leads that closely align with their ICP and are more likely to convert, they reduce the cost of marketing to unqualified leads and save on marketing expenses.

Strategies for Improving Lead Quality in B2B ABM

Now, let's discuss strategies for improving lead quality in your B2B ABM efforts:

Refine Your Ideal Customer Profile (ICP): A well-defined ICP is critical for attracting high-quality leads. Regularly review and refine your ICP based on your experiences and the evolving needs of your business.

Collaborate with Sales: Work closely with your sales team to define what constitutes a high-quality lead. Their insights can be invaluable in shaping your lead generation and nurturing strategies.

Segment Your Audience: Segment your target accounts and leads based on their fit with your ICP, engagement level, and other criteria. This allows you to tailor your messaging and outreach more effectively.

Implement Lead Scoring: Use lead scoring systems to assess the quality of leads based on predetermined criteria objectively. Assign scores to leads to identify those that are most likely to convert.

Leverage Intent Data: Monitor the online behavior and signals provided by leads to gauge their intent. Leads showing strong intent are often of higher quality and should be prioritized.

Tailor Content for Each Stage: Create content that addresses the specific needs and concerns of leads at each stage of the buyer's journey. This ensures that leads receive relevant information as they progress through the sales funnel.

Use Personalization: Personalize your outreach to leads to make them feel valued and understood. Personalized communication can significantly boost lead quality.

Implement Progressive Profiling: Instead of requesting all information upfront, use progressive profiling to collect data from leads gradually. This minimizes friction in the lead generation process and ensures that leads are more qualified.

Common Challenges in Lead Quality Management

While lead quality is a crucial aspect of B2B ABM, managing it effectively can present some challenges. Here are a few common issues:

- **Data Quality:** Inaccurate or outdated data can lead to targeting the wrong leads or accounts, diminishing lead quality.

- **Alignment between Sales and Marketing:** Poor alignment can result in differences in defining high-quality leads, leading to misaligned efforts.

Lead Volume: Striking the right balance between lead quality and lead volume can be challenging. Continuously analyze the leads that convert to successful sales opportunities and the ones that are lost. Identify patterns during the sales process and update your marketing and sales process around the successful deals.

CHAPTER 11

MANAGING ENHANCED CUSTOMER RELATIONSHIPS

Fostering Stronger Relationships Between B2B Marketers and Their Target Accounts Is Key

In the world of B2B marketing, building and nurturing strong relationships between marketers and their target accounts is a cornerstone of success. These relationships are vital for understanding the needs of your clients, providing value, and ultimately driving growth. In this chapter, we'll explore what it means to foster stronger relationships between B2B marketers and their target accounts and provide five effective examples of how to accomplish this.

What It Means to Foster Stronger Relationships

Fostering stronger relationships between B2B marketers and their target accounts goes beyond just transactions or sales. It involves building trust, understanding the unique needs and challenges of each account, and creating a lasting connection that can lead to mutually beneficial partnerships. The following key elements often characterize this process:

- **Personalization:** Understanding that each target account is unique and tailoring your communication and offerings to meet their specific needs and goals.
- **Active Listening:** Engaging in meaningful two-way communication, where you not only convey your message but also listen to the account's feedback and concerns.
- **Empathy:** Showing that you understand the account's challenges and demonstrating a genuine interest in helping them overcome those challenges.
- **Consistency:** Maintaining a consistent and reliable presence in the account's journey, ensuring that they can count on you to deliver value and support.
- **Value Delivery:** Providing solutions, insights, and resources that are genuinely helpful to the account, even before a purchase is made.
- **Long-term Focus:** Recognizing that building strong relationships is not about quick wins but about establishing enduring partnerships that can result in repeated business and advocacy.

Now, let's explore five effective examples of how to foster stronger relationships between B2B marketers and their target accounts.

Example 1: Customized Content and Engagement

One of the most powerful ways to build strong relationships with target accounts is through the creation of customized content and personalized engagement strategies. This approach involves tailoring your marketing content and outreach efforts to the specific needs and challenges of each account. Here's how to do it effectively:

- **Content Personalization:** Create content that speaks directly to the challenges and goals of each target account. This may include custom whitepapers, case studies, industry-specific reports, and personalized messages from your team.
- **Personalized Outreach:** Use personalized email marketing, social media engagement, and direct outreach to connect with individuals within the target accounts. The messaging should reflect a deep understanding of their situation and a desire to provide solutions.
- **Webinars and Workshops:** Host webinars or virtual workshops that address the specific concerns of your target accounts. These events allow for direct interaction and the sharing of valuable insights.
- **Customized Demos and Trials:** If applicable, provide customized product demos or trial versions of your offerings that are tailored to the needs of the target accounts.
- **Continuous Engagement:** Don't limit your interaction to a single campaign. Nurture the relationship with ongoing communication, sharing valuable resources, and staying engaged with the account's progress.

Example Scenario:

A software company is targeting large enterprise accounts for their project management software. They create custom case studies showcasing how their software improved project efficiency in the same industry as the target accounts. In addition, they conduct personalized webinars to address specific project management challenges faced by each account.

Example 2: Account-Specific Strategies

Fostering strong relationships involves recognizing that each target account may require a unique marketing strategy. One-size-fits-all approaches are less effective in B2B marketing. Here's how to create account-specific strategies effectively:

- **Account Analysis:** Conduct a thorough analysis of each target account, considering factors such as industry, company size, current challenges, and position in the buying journey.
- **Tailored Messaging:** Develop messaging that aligns with the specific needs and pain points of each account. This messaging should be consistent across all marketing channels and campaigns.
- **Multichannel Approach:** Implement a multichannel marketing approach that caters to the preferences and behaviors of each account. This may include email marketing, social media advertising, webinars, direct outreach, and more.
- **Industry Insights:** Provide account-specific industry insights and reports to demonstrate your expertise and understanding of their market.

- **Coordinated Efforts:** Ensure that your sales and marketing teams are aligned in their approach to each target account. Sales should be equipped with the tools and information needed to engage effectively.

Example Scenario:

A marketing agency is targeting accounts in the healthcare industry. They create customized strategies for each account based on their unique challenges. This includes industry-specific content, email campaigns, and webinars. The sales team collaborates with the marketing team to ensure a coordinated effort.

Example 3: Personalization at Scale

While personalization is crucial, achieving it at scale is a common challenge for B2B marketers. To foster strong relationships, you need to strike a balance between personalized communication and efficiency. Here's how to personalize at scale effectively:

- **Segmentation:** Divide your target accounts into segments based on shared characteristics, such as industry, role, or stage in the buying journey.
- **Dynamic Content:** Utilize marketing automation tools to create dynamic content that adapts based on the characteristics of each segment.
- **Behavioral Triggers:** Set up behavioral triggers that respond to the actions of target accounts, such as visiting specific web pages or engaging with particular content.
- **Personalized Email Campaigns:** Develop email campaigns that address the specific pain points and goals of each segment.

- **Scalable Personalization Tools:** Invest in personalization tools that can automate and streamline the process of tailoring content and outreach.

Example Scenario:

A software company uses marketing automation to personalize its email campaigns. Based on the segment (e.g., current customers, prospects, leads), the email content adapts to provide relevant information and calls to action. This scalable personalization approach ensures that each account receives customized messaging.

Example 4: Continuous Communication and Education

Strong relationships are built on trust and consistent communication. It's essential to maintain an ongoing dialogue with your target accounts and provide them with educational resources. Here's how to accomplish this:

- **Newsletters:** Send regular newsletters that share industry insights, company updates, and relevant content.
- **Webinars and Workshops:** Host webinars and workshops that provide educational content and an opportunity for direct interaction.
- **Content Hubs:** Create content hubs or resource centers where target accounts can access valuable materials on-demand.
- **Account Reviews:** Periodically review the progress and challenges of target accounts and offer insights or suggestions for improvement.
- **Feedback Loop:** Encourage target accounts to provide feedback and suggestions, showing that you value their input.

Example Scenario:

A B2B SaaS company maintains ongoing communication with its target accounts through monthly newsletters, webinars, and an online resource center. They also conduct quarterly account reviews to assess progress and offer guidance.

Example 5: Thought Leadership and Expertise Sharing

Establishing your brand as a thought leader and sharing your expertise can significantly contribute to building strong relationships with target accounts. Here's how to accomplish this effectively:

- **Create Thought Leadership Content:** Develop content that positions your company as a thought leader in your industry. This might include whitepapers, research reports, or industry-specific insights.
- **Guest Speaking and Panels:** Participate in industry events, webinars, or panel discussions to showcase your expertise.
- **Educational Blog Posts:** Publish blog posts.
- **Contribute to industry publications:** Identify your industry publications and build relationships with the publisher and editor of the publication. Consider writing 1500-to-2000-word articles about industry topics that can be published as a contributing writer.

CHAPTER 12

HOW TO HAVE ROBUST RETURN ON INVESTMENT (ROI)

The precise targeting, personalization, and improved lead quality associated with ABM contribute to a better ROI.

How Precise Targeting, Personalization, and Improved Lead Quality in ABM Contribute to Better ROI?

effective strategy for businesses but the analytics that are implemented with your marketing programs can help you to maximize their return on investment (ROI). ABM's success hinges on its ability to deliver precise targeting, personalization, and improved lead quality. In this comprehensive guide, we'll explore how these elements contribute to better ROI in ABM and provide five real-world examples to illustrate their impact.

Power of Precise Targeting in ABM

Precise targeting is at the core of ABM and it involves identifying and focusing on a select group of high-value accounts that have the potential to drive substantial revenue for your business.

Instead of casting a wide net, ABM narrows the focus to ensure that marketing efforts are concentrated on the accounts most likely to convert. Here's how precise targeting contributes to better ROI:

- **Resource Efficiency:** Precise targeting allows you to allocate your resources effectively. Your marketing and sales teams can concentrate their efforts on a smaller number of accounts, making the best use of their time and resources.
- **Higher Conversion Rates:** By concentrating on high-potential accounts, you increase the likelihood of conversion. These accounts are more likely to engage with your content and move through the sales funnel.
- **Shorter Sales Cycles:** When you target accounts that closely align with your ideal customer profile, the sales cycle tends to be shorter. The accounts are already a good fit for your offerings, reducing the need for extensive education or persuasion.
- **Reduced Waste:** With precise targeting, you avoid marketing to accounts that are not a good fit for your business. This minimizes wasted resources on unqualified leads or accounts that are unlikely to convert.
- **Personalization:** Precise targeting makes it easier to personalize your marketing efforts as you can tailor your messaging and content to address the specific needs and challenges of each account.

Example 1: A software company that provides Enterprise Resource Planning (ERP) Solutions identifies a select group of Fortune 500 companies in the manufacturing sector as high-value accounts. By precisely targeting these accounts, they focus their marketing and sales efforts on engaging this specific group, resulting in a higher ROI.

The Role of Personalization in ABM

Personalization is another critical element of ABM. It involves crafting customized messages and content that directly address the unique needs and challenges of individual target accounts. Here's how personalization contributes to better ROI:

- **Increased Engagement:** Personalized content is more engaging because it speaks directly to the account's specific concerns and goals. Decision-makers are more likely to pay attention to and interact with content that resonates with their situation.
- **Improved Conversion Rates:** Personalization enhances the likelihood of conversion. When your messaging resonates with the account's challenges and needs, they are more likely to take action, such as requesting more information or making a purchase.
- **Enhanced Customer Relationships:** Personalization fosters stronger customer relationships. By demonstrating a deep understanding of the account's needs and providing tailored solutions, you build trust and credibility which are crucial in the B2B sales process.
- **Reduced Waste:** Personalization ensures that your marketing resources are spent on efforts that are more likely to convert. You're not sending generic messages to accounts that are not a good fit for your offering.
- **Brand Differentiation:** In a competitive B2B landscape, personalization sets you apart from competitors. It

positions your brand as one that genuinely understands and caters to the unique needs of your target accounts.

Example 2: A marketing agency uses personalization in its ABM campaign for a group of financial institutions. They create customized content that addresses the specific challenges faced by each institution, such as regulatory compliance and risk management. This personalized approach results in higher engagement and conversion rates.

The Impact of Improved Lead Quality in ABM

Improved lead quality is a direct result of precise targeting and personalization in ABM. It means that the leads you generate and engage with are more likely to convert and become valuable customers. **Here's how improved lead quality contributes to better ROI:**

- **Higher Conversion Rates:** High-quality leads are more likely to convert into customers. They closely match your ideal customer profile which means they are a good fit for your offerings and have a higher propensity to buy.
- **Shorter Sales Cycles:** Improved lead quality often results in shorter sales cycles. Since high-quality leads are well-aligned with your offerings, they require less time for education and decision-making.
- **Increased Customer Lifetime Value (CLV):** High-quality leads not only convert but are also more likely to remain engaged with your business over time. They may make repeat purchases and become loyal customers, contributing to a higher CLV.

- **Cost Savings:** By focusing on lead quality, you reduce the costs associated with generating and nurturing unqualified leads. This efficient allocation of resources leads to cost savings.
- **Word-of-Mouth Referrals:** Satisfied, high-quality leads who become customers are more likely to recommend your brand to others in their network, resulting in word-of-mouth referrals and potential new business opportunities.

Example 3:

An IT services company targeting mid-sized businesses utilizes improved lead quality in its ABM strategy. By precisely targeting accounts in need of IT support and personalizing their outreach with tailored solutions, they generate high-quality leads that have shorter sales cycles and a higher CLV.

Here are some additional examples that showcase how precise targeting, personalization, and improved lead quality work together to enhance ROI in ABM.

Example 4:

A cybersecurity company focuses on precise targeting by identifying accounts in highly regulated industries, like healthcare and finance, as their ideal customers. They create personalized content and outreach strategies that address the specific compliance and security needs of these accounts. This approach results in improved lead quality, as accounts engaged are already interested in solutions that meet their industry-specific challenges, leading to higher conversion rates and a better ROI.

Example 5:

A marketing automation software provider uses precise targeting to narrow down accounts based on company size and marketing needs. They personalize their messaging by offering tailored solutions for accounts with different requirements, such as lead generation, email automation, or analytics. This personalization leads to higher-quality leads, as the accounts engage with content that directly addresses their pain points. This, in turn, results in shorter sales cycles and a better ROI, as the leads are more likely to convert.

The combination of precise targeting, personalization, and improved lead quality in ABM is a powerful recipe for achieving a better ROI. These elements ensure that your marketing and sales efforts are focused on the right accounts, with messaging that resonates with their specific needs. This results in higher engagement, improved conversion rates, shorter sales cycles, increased customer lifetime value, cost savings, and the potential for word-of-mouth referrals. Ultimately, this approach not only enhances the bottom line but also establishes lasting, mutually beneficial relationships with your target accounts.

CHAPTER 13

BUILDING A SCALABILITY AND ADAPTABILITY MARKETING PROGRAM

ABM strategies can be scaled to fit the specific needs of your business.

Scalability and Adaptability in B2B ABM Strategies

Account-Based Marketing (ABM) is designed to enable marketers the ability to precisely target specific organizations, functional areas of the organizations, and specific titles with highly personalized content. However, the successful implementation of ABM relies on both, scalability and adaptability. While scalability allows businesses to extend the reach of their ABM efforts, adaptability ensures that these strategies can be tailored to specific needs. In this chapter, we'll explain what scalability and adaptability mean in ABM and provide four detailed examples of how these concepts can be applied effectively.

Understanding Scalability in ABM

Scalability in ABM refers to the capacity to expand and adjust your ABM strategies to accommodate a larger number of target accounts without compromising the quality and effectiveness of your marketing efforts. It's essential because as your business grows, you may want to target more accounts or enter new markets. Here are key aspects of scalability in ABM:

- **Increased Account Volume:** Scalable ABM strategies should allow you to add more target accounts to your campaigns, ensuring you can pursue multiple opportunities without overwhelming your resources.
- **Resource Efficiency:** Despite the expansion in the number of accounts, your ABM strategies should still make efficient use of your resources, including marketing budgets and personnel.
- **Consistency:** Scalability requires maintaining consistent messaging and personalization across all accounts, even as the volume increases. It's important that the quality of engagement remains high.
- **Integration with Technology:** The use of technology, such as marketing automation platforms and CRM systems, is essential for scaling ABM. These tools help manage larger account lists and automate processes.

Now, let's delve into four detailed examples of how scalability can be achieved in ABM:

Example 1: Segmenting Target Accounts

A B2B software company initially targets a small number of high-value accounts in the healthcare industry. As they look to scale their efforts, they realize that they can't engage with all healthcare accounts at the same level of personalization. Instead, they segment healthcare accounts into tiers based on potential value and engagement level. They reserve highly personalized ABM campaigns for top-tier accounts while implementing more automated and less resource-intensive approaches for lower-tier accounts. This segmentation allows them to maintain scalability while tailoring their strategies to different segments.

Example 2: Account-Based Advertising

An IT services provider plans to scale its ABM efforts by targeting a larger number of accounts in the technology sector. To do this, they leverage account-based advertising platforms that enable them to display personalized ads to their target accounts. These ads are based on the specific industry, challenges, or needs of each account. By automating the advertising process and tailoring the content, they can effectively target a larger volume of accounts without significantly increasing their manual workload, ensuring scalability.

Example 3: Automation for Outreach

A marketing agency specializing in content marketing initially focuses on a small set of accounts. To scale their ABM efforts, they implement marketing automation tools that allow them to automate various aspects of their outreach. For instance, they use marketing automation to send personalized email campaigns to a larger volume of target accounts. The platform enables them to segment accounts, trigger emails based on account behavior, and maintain consistent messaging. This automation streamlines their outreach process and supports scalability.

Example 4: Predictive Analytics for Lead Scoring

A cybersecurity company starts its ABM journey by targeting a select group of accounts in the financial sector. As they look to expand their reach, they implement predictive analytics to help prioritize and score leads. Predictive analytics consider various data points such as account behavior, firmographics, and engagement history, to assign scores to leads. This allows the company to identify the most promising leads among a larger set of target accounts. By focusing their efforts on high-scoring leads, they can efficiently scale their ABM campaigns.

Understanding Adaptability in ABM

Adaptability in ABM means the capability of the program to be able to adjust and fine-tune your strategies to meet the specific needs and challenges of your target accounts. Along the way, you will identify what is working and what is not. And you need to have the ability to pivot and continuously optimize the program. Recognize that not all accounts are the same, and the ability to customize your approach is crucial for success. Here are key aspects of adaptability in ABM:

- Tailoring Messaging: An adaptable ABM strategy should allow for the creation of personalized messages and content that directly address the unique needs and pain points of individual accounts.
- Flexibility in Campaigns: Adaptability means having the flexibility to modify campaigns, channels, and tactics to align with the preferences and behaviors of each account.
- Account-Specific Goals: It's important to set specific goals for each account based on their challenges and

objectives, rather than applying a one-size-fits-all approach.

- Feedback Integration: Adaptability should involve the ability to incorporate feedback from accounts into your strategy, making adjustments based on their input and engagement.

Now, let's explore four detailed examples of how adaptability can be applied effectively in ABM:

Example 1: Customized Content Creation

A marketing agency provides services to a diverse range of B2B clients. To adapt their ABM strategy to the unique needs of each account, they offer customized content creation. For instance, they create industry-specific blog posts, whitepapers, and case studies that directly address the challenges faced by each client. By tailoring their content, they demonstrate their understanding of the account's specific industry and needs, resulting in a more adaptable ABM approach.

Example 2: Account-Specific Webinars

A SaaS company offers a range of software solutions. To adapt their ABM strategy, they host account-specific webinars. These webinars are tailored to address the precise challenges and objectives of each target account. For instance, if one account is interested in improving data analytics, the webinar focuses on that topic. Another account focused on security receives a webinar discussing cybersecurity solutions. This adaptability allows them to deliver highly relevant and engaging content to each account.

Example 3: Dynamic Campaigns

A business technology provider uses adaptability in their ABM campaigns by creating dynamic campaigns that respond to the behavior and engagement of target accounts. For instance, if an account shows significant interest in a particular product or service, the campaign adjusts to provide more in-depth information on that offering. Conversely, if an account is less engaged, the campaign may emphasize educational content to address their specific needs. This adaptability ensures that campaigns align with the preferences and behaviors of each account.

Example 4: Feedback-Driven Personalization

A manufacturing company takes an adaptable approach in its ABM strategy by actively seeking feedback from target accounts. They regularly solicit input on their products and services, as well as the content and communication provided. This feedback is used to refine and adapt their ABM approach. If an account expresses interest in specific features or improvements, the company incorporates these suggestions into its product offerings and marketing messages. This adaptability, based on feedback, fosters stronger relationships with accounts and drives better ROI.

How to Scale and Adapt ABM Strategies to Fit Specific Needs

To successfully scale and adapt your ABM strategies to meet the specific needs of your business, consider the following steps:

- Define Your Ideal Customer Profile (ICP): Start by clearly defining your ICP. This will help you target the right accounts from the beginning.
- Segment Your Accounts: Divide your target accounts into segments based on shared characteristics such as industry, company size, and specific needs.
- Leverage Technology: Invest in marketing automation platforms, predictive analytics, and account-based advertising.

CHAPTER 14

ACCOUNT-BASED MARKETING EFFECTIVE IN COMPLEX SALES CYCLES

ABM is particularly effective in industries with complex and lengthy sales cycles.

While ABM can be applied across various industries, it is particularly effective in verticals characterized by complex selling and lengthy sales cycles. In this chapter, we'll explain why ABM is highly effective in such industries and provide five real-world examples to illustrate its impact.

Understanding ABM in Complex and Lengthy Sales Cycles

Before diving into the effectiveness of ABM in industries with complex and lengthy sales cycles, it's essential to understand the core principles of ABM, so I am going to emphasize the core values of ABM:

Account-Based Marketing is a strategic approach that focuses on identifying and targeting high-value accounts, rather than casting a wide net to capture leads. It involves the alignment of sales and marketing efforts to personalize outreach, nurture relationships, and drive engagement within these target accounts.

Complex and Lengthy Sales Cycles:

Industries with complex and lengthy sales cycles are characterized by extended decision-making processes, multiple stakeholders, and significant investments. These industries often include sectors like enterprise software, healthcare, finance, manufacturing, and telecommunications.

Now, let's delve into why ABM is particularly effective in industries with complex and lengthy sales cycles:

Targeted Engagement:

ABM allows businesses to target their marketing efforts precisely at key accounts. In industries with intricate sales cycles, where multiple decision-makers and influencers are involved, precision is critical. By concentrating resources on a select group of high-value accounts, ABM ensures that every interaction is meaningful and tailored to the unique needs of each account.

Example 1: A B2B software company focuses its ABM efforts on large healthcare organizations for its patient management system. By identifying and targeting specific accounts, they can tailor their messaging to address the complex compliance and integration challenges inherent in the healthcare industry.

Relationship Building:

In lengthy sales cycles, relationships are paramount. ABM fosters strong, personalized relationships with target accounts over time. Marketing and sales teams work together to engage, educate, and support accounts through their journey. These relationships build trust, which is especially critical in industries where investments are substantial, and decisions have long-term consequences.

Example 2: An industrial equipment manufacturer in a complex industry targets a large manufacturing plant. Their ABM strategy includes personalized outreach, on-site visits, and educational content to build trust and strengthen relationships. Over time, these relationships result in substantial equipment orders.

Customized Content:

ABM enables the creation of highly customized content that directly addresses the challenges, concerns, and goals of each target account. In industries with intricate sales cycles, where account-specific nuances matter, this level of customization is invaluable. It allows businesses to demonstrate their deep understanding of an account's unique needs.

Example 3: A marketing agency provides services to a variety of B2B clients with diverse industries and goals. Using ABM, they create customized content for each client, addressing their specific challenges and objectives. This customization showcases their expertise and resonates with the unique needs of each account.

Multi-Channel Engagement:

In industries with complex sales cycles, decision-makers and influencers engage with content across various channels and at different stages. ABM allows for multi-channel engagement, delivering a consistent message through channels such as email, social media, webinars, and personalized content hubs. This comprehensive approach ensures that all stakeholders receive relevant information.

Example 4: A telecommunications company targets large enterprises in its ABM strategy. They employ multi-channel engagement, combining personalized email campaigns, social media engagement, webinars, and personalized resource hubs. This approach caters to the various roles and preferences within the target accounts.

Consistency and Long-term Focus:

Industries with complex and lengthy sales cycles often involve extended nurturing periods. ABM's consistent and long-term approach aligns with these needs. The strategy isn't just about quick wins; it's about building enduring relationships with target accounts that may result in repeated business and advocacy.

Example 5: A healthcare IT provider targets hospitals and clinics. They use ABM to nurture relationships over extended periods, providing consistent support and educational content. This long-term focus results in accounts repeatedly turning to them for new technological solutions as their needs evolve.

Examples of ABM Effectiveness in Complex and Lengthy Sales Cycles

Let's explore five real-world examples that demonstrate the effectiveness of ABM in industries with complex and lengthy sales cycles:

Example 1: Healthcare Software Provider

A healthcare software provider targets large hospital networks for its Electronic Health Record (EHR) system. Given the complex nature of healthcare systems and the lengthy procurement process, they implement ABM to engage with key decision-makers and influencers within each target hospital. By providing personalized content, conducting webinars on healthcare compliance, and facilitating in-person demonstrations, they build strong relationships that span the entire procurement cycle which can extend over several months. ABM allows them to focus their resources on high-value accounts and navigate the intricate decision-making landscape. As a result, they secure multi-million-dollar contracts and build long-term partnerships with major hospital networks.

Example 2: Financial Services Firm

A financial services firm specializing in wealth management caters to high-net-worth individuals and family offices. In the finance industry, where trust and personal relationships are paramount, they leverage ABM to build trust with their clients. Their ABM approach involves personalized outreach, exclusive events, and thought leadership content. By tailoring their communication to individual client goals and concerns, they nurture long-term relationships that span years. The lengthy sales cycle in wealth management necessitates ongoing education and trust-building and ABM provides the ideal framework for this approach. The firm not only retains clients but also receives referrals, resulting in substantial assets under management.

Example 3: Enterprise IT Solutions Provider

An enterprise IT solutions provider targets large corporations and government agencies for its cybersecurity solutions. These organizations often have complex procurement processes, extensive security assessments, and a multitude of stakeholders. The company employs ABM to address the unique challenges faced by each target account. Their strategy includes creating customized content addressing specific security concerns, engaging with key IT decision-makers, and facilitating technical demonstrations. ABM's precision allows them to navigate the intricate sales cycle of enterprise cybersecurity and build confidence among security-conscious organizations. As a result, they secure multi-year contracts with major corporations and government agencies.

Example 4: Aerospace Manufacturer

An aerospace manufacturer focuses its ABM efforts on major airlines for its aircraft components. The sales cycle in the aerospace industry is not only lengthy but also involves stringent safety standards and regulations. The company tailors its ABM strategy to address the unique requirements of each airline, including safety compliance, component durability, and industry-specific certifications. They engage with technical and procurement teams, provide specialized content on component testing, and offer on-site visits to manufacturing facilities. This personalized approach is vital in industries where safety and compliance are paramount. As a result, they secure multi-million-dollar contracts with major airlines and maintain long-term relationships that span the lifecycle of aircraft fleets.

Example 5: Biotechnology Company

A biotechnology company specializing in pharmaceutical research targets large pharmaceutical companies and research institutions. In the biotech industry, where research and development processes can take years, they implement ABM to engage with key scientists, researchers, and procurement teams. Their ABM approach includes creating content that outlines specific-use cases and how the technology or solution can help to improve operational efficiencies, reduce cost, and support business requirements such as compliance.

CHAPTER 15

HOW TO IMPLEMENT DATA-DRIVEN DECISION-MAKING

ABM relies on data and analytics to evaluate campaign performance and make necessary adjustments.

Leveraging data and analytics in Account-Based Marketing to track and evaluate the performance of your ABM is essential. In this chapter, we will discuss what type of data and analytics you should manage. A key driver of ABM's success is its reliance on data and analytics to evaluate campaign performance and make necessary adjustments. Now, let's explore how data and analytics play a pivotal role in ABM, why they are crucial for campaign optimization, and provide five real-world examples of how ABM strategies have harnessed the power of data and analytics to deliver impressive results.

The Foundation of Data and Analytics in ABM

Before delving into the specifics of data and analytics in ABM, we must understand the central role in the strategy:

- Data: In ABM, data refers to the information collected about target accounts, including firmographics, intent

data, engagement data, and historical data. This data serves as the foundation for identifying and segmenting target accounts and understanding their behavior and preferences.
- Analytics: Analytics, in the context of ABM, involves the use of data to extract insights, patterns, and trends. Analytics enable marketers to measure the effectiveness of their campaigns, identify areas for improvement, and make data-driven decisions.

The Role of Data and Analytics in ABM

Data and analytics in ABM serve several critical functions:

- Identifying Target Accounts: Data is used to identify and select target accounts that align with the organization's ideal customer profile (ICP), ensuring that resources are allocated to the most promising accounts.
- Personalization: Data provides insights into the unique needs and preferences of target accounts, enabling the creation of personalized content and messaging.
- Measurement and KPIs: Analytics help define key performance indicators (KPIs) and measure campaign performance against these metrics. This includes tracking engagement, lead generation, conversion rates, and return on investment (ROI).
- Segmentation: Data allows for the segmentation of target accounts into different categories based on factors such as industry, company size, or behavior, which in turn informs personalized content and outreach.

- Lead Scoring: Analytics are used to score leads within target accounts, indicating their level of engagement and readiness to progress through the sales funnel.
- Campaign Optimization: Data and analytics guide campaign optimization by providing insights into what is working and what needs adjustment. This iterative process helps marketers refine their strategies over time.

Now, let's explore five real-world examples of how data and analytics are harnessed in ABM for performance evaluation and adaptation:

Example 1: Predictive Analytics for Account Selection

A B2B software company utilizes predictive analytics to identify high-value target accounts for its cloud-based solutions. By analyzing historical data, the company develops a predictive model that scores accounts based on their likelihood to convert and their potential lifetime value. This data-driven approach allows the company to allocate resources to accounts with the highest predictive scores, ensuring a more efficient and effective ABM strategy. As a result, they witness an increase in engagement and conversions from their top-tier accounts.

Example 2: Behavioral Analytics for Personalization

A marketing automation platform provider focuses on a wide range of target accounts in various industries. To personalize their outreach effectively, they employ behavioral analytics. By tracking website interactions, email engagement, and content downloads, they gain insights into the specific interests and needs of each account. This data informs the creation of personalized email campaigns and content recommendations tailored to individual account behavior. The result is significantly higher click-through rates and a boost in overall engagement.

Example 3: Intent Data for Content Relevance

A cybersecurity solutions provider aims to engage with financial institutions for its threat detection software. To ensure content relevance, they leverage intent data, which indicates when target accounts are actively researching security solutions. By monitoring online behaviors and keyword searches, they identify accounts showing strong intent to invest in cybersecurity. This data-driven approach enables them to deliver timely and relevant content, such as webinars and whitepapers, addressing the specific concerns of these accounts. As a result, they experience higher conversion rates and accelerated sales cycles.

Example 4: Lead Scoring and Progression

A medical device manufacturer pursues target accounts in the healthcare sector. To manage their complex and lengthy sales cycles effectively, they implement lead scoring and progression based on data and analytics. They score leads within each account based on their engagement levels and readiness to make a purchase. As leads progress through the sales funnel, the company adjusts its outreach and content to align with the stage of the buying journey. This data-driven lead progression results in shorter sales cycles and an increase in conversion rates.

Example 5: Campaign Attribution and ROI Measurement

An enterprise IT solutions provider uses ABM to target large corporations and government agencies. They employ data and analytics to attribute the impact of their ABM campaigns to specific revenue generation. By tracking the entire customer journey, from initial engagement to closed deals, they gain a comprehensive understanding of which campaigns and touchpoints contribute most to revenue. This data-driven attribution model allows them to allocate their marketing budget to the most effective strategies and channels. They achieve a significant improvement in ROI and a higher proportion of closed-won deals.

ABM Data and Analytics Framework

To successfully leverage data and analytics in your ABM strategy, consider the following framework:

- Data Collection: Ensure you have a robust data collection process in place to gather information about target accounts. This may include data on firmographics, behavior, intent, and engagement.

- Data Integration: Integrate data from various sources, such as CRM systems, marketing automation platforms, and third-party data providers, to create a unified view of your target accounts.

- Segmentation: Use data to segment target accounts into categories based on specific criteria, such as industry, company size, and engagement level. This segmentation guides the creation of personalized content and outreach.

- Personalization: Tailor your messaging and content to align with the unique needs and preferences of each segmented group. Personalization enhances engagement and resonates with the target accounts.

- Analytics and KPIs: Define key performance indicators (KPIs) that align with your campaign objectives. Use

analytics to measure performance against these KPIs, track engagement, and identify areas for improvement.
- Lead Scoring: Implement lead scoring models that leverage data to determine the readiness of leads to progress through the sales funnel, which ensures that leads are appropriately nurtured based on their behavior.
- Campaign Optimization: Continuously analyze the data and analytics to optimize your ABM campaigns. Identify successful strategies, adjust tactics that aren't yielding results, and refine your approach based on data-driven insights.

Continuous Monitoring and Optimization of your ABM program

ABM is not a one-time endeavor but a continuous cycle of improvement. Data and analytics provide the foundation for this iterative process. By collecting, analyzing, and acting on data-driven insights, organizations can fine-tune their ABM strategies, adapt to evolving customer needs, and achieve more impactful results. As industries shift, customer behavior changes and competition intensifies, the power of data and analytics in ABM becomes increasingly indispensable for success.

CHAPTER 16

INTENT DATA AND ACCOUNT-BASED MARKETING

Intent data in the context of B2B marketing refers to information that indicates a potential customer's interest or intention to make a purchase. It provides insights into the online behavior of businesses and individuals, revealing their activities and engagements across digital channels. This data is crucial for marketers as it helps them understand the needs and preferences of potential customers, allowing for more targeted and effective marketing efforts.

There are two main types of intent data:

- First-Party Intent Data: This is data collected directly from your digital properties, such as your website, emails, or webinars. It includes information like website visits, content downloads, and interactions with your marketing materials. Analyzing this data helps you understand the behavior of your existing leads and customers.
- Third-Party Intent Data: This data is collected from external sources, often through partnerships with data

providers. It includes information about the online behavior of prospects on websites, industry forums, and other digital platforms, even if they haven't directly interacted with your brand. Third-party intent data provides a broader view of the market and helps identify potential prospects who may not be in your immediate network.

How Intent Data is Leveraged in B2B Marketing:

- Personalized Messaging: By analyzing intent data, marketers can tailor their messaging to align with the specific needs and interests of potential customers. This personalization increases the relevance of marketing communications, making it more likely that the message will resonate with the target audience.

- Lead Scoring and Prioritization: Intent data is valuable for lead scoring, helping marketers identify and prioritize leads that are more likely to convert. Leads showing higher levels of engagement and interest, as indicated by their online behavior, can be given higher scores and treated as a priority for sales outreach.

Account-Based Marketing (ABM):

Intent data is beneficial in account-based marketing strategies. It helps identify accounts that are actively researching or showing interest in relevant topics, allowing marketers to focus their efforts on those accounts with a higher likelihood of conversion.

- Content Strategy Optimization: Marketers can use intent data to optimize their content strategy. By understanding the topics and types of content that resonate with their

audience, they can create more targeted and relevant content, improving engagement and conversion rates.
- Sales and Marketing Alignment: Intent data facilitates better collaboration between sales and marketing teams. Sales teams can use the insights gained from intent data to have more informed and meaningful conversations with prospects, increasing the chances of closing deals.

In summary, intent data in B2B marketing is a powerful tool for understanding and predicting customer behavior. It allows businesses to optimize their strategies, improve targeting, and ultimately drive more successful marketing campaigns.

Implementing Intent Data in Account-Based Marketing

Implementing intent data in an account-based marketing (ABM) program involves a strategic and systematic approach to leverage insights into the behaviors and interests of target accounts. Below, I'll provide a detailed guide with examples of how to implement intent data in ABM:

1. **Define Your ABM Strategy:**

   Before diving into intent data implementation, it's crucial to have a well-defined ABM strategy, including identifying target accounts, understanding their pain points, and aligning sales and marketing teams. Let's consider an example:

Example: A company named Smith, a B2B tech firm, has decided to focus on a select group of enterprise accounts in the healthcare sector for its ABM program. The goal is to provide personalized solutions addressing the specific needs of these high-value accounts.

2. Select the Right Intent Data Sources:

Identify and select the intent data sources that align with your ABM goals. First-party data from your marketing automation platform and website analytics can be combined with third-party intent data from specialized providers. Example:

Example: Company XYZ subscribes to a third-party intent data provider that monitors online activities related to healthcare technology. This provider tracks signals such as website visits, content downloads, and social media engagements within the target accounts.

3. Integrate Intent Data with Your CRM and Marketing Automation Platform:

For effective use, integrate intent data with your Customer Relationship Management (CRM) system and marketing automation platform. This integration ensures seamless communication between sales and marketing teams and allows for automated workflows triggered by intent signals.

Example: Intent data from the third-party provider is integrated into Company Smith's CRM and marketing automation platform. Whenever a target account exhibits strong intent signals, the sales team receives automated alerts, prompting them to take immediate action.

4. Segment Your Target Accounts Based on Intent Signals:

Use the intent data to segment your target accounts based on their level of engagement and interest. This segmentation allows for more personalized and targeted outreach strategies.

Example: Company name Smith categorizes its target accounts into three segments based on intent signals: 'High Intent,' 'Moderate Intent,' and 'Low Intent.' High Intent accounts are actively researching and engaging, while Moderate and Low Intent accounts require different nurturing approaches.

5. Develop Personalized Content:

Craft content that resonates with the specific interests and pain points of each account segment. Leverage the insights from intent data to create content that addresses the topics and challenges relevant to your target accounts.

Example: For Intent accounts, Company XYZ creates in-depth whitepapers and case studies showcasing the impact of their solutions in the healthcare sector. Moderate and Low Intent accounts receive more general content introducing the company's expertise and capabilities.

6. Deploy Targeted Advertising Campaigns:

Utilize intent data to run targeted advertising campaigns. This ensures that your ads reach the right people at the right time, increasing the chances of engagement.

Example: Using intent data, the company Smith runs targeted LinkedIn ads specifically aimed at individuals within the target accounts who have shown interest in healthcare technology solutions. *The ad content is aligned with the intent signals, emphasizing relevant features and benefits.*

7. Implement Personalized Email Campaigns:

Craft personalized email campaigns that speak directly to the interests and needs of each account segment. Intent data is used to tailor email content and messaging.

Example: Company Acme's marketing team sends personalized emails to contacts within High Intent accounts, referencing recent activities and expressing a deep understanding of their specific challenges. For Moderate and Low Intent accounts, the emails focus on gradually building awareness and interest.

8. Enable Sales Teams with Intent Insights:

Equip your sales teams with the insights derived from intent data. Provide them with the necessary training to interpret intent signals and tailor their conversations accordingly.

Example: Whenever a High Intent signal is detected, the sales team at Company Acme receives real-time alerts and detailed reports on the prospect's recent interactions. This enables them to engage in timely and relevant conversations with potential clients.

9. Continuous Monitoring and Optimization:

Implement a system for continuous monitoring of intent signals and regularly optimize your ABM strategy based on the evolving interests and behaviors of your target accounts.

Example: Company Acme regularly reviews and updates its intent data strategy. If there are shifts in the topics of interest within the healthcare sector, the marketing team adjusts its content and messaging to stay aligned with the changing landscape.

10. Measure and Analyze Results:

Implement key performance indicators (KPIs) to measure the success of your intent-based ABM program. Analyze the data regularly to identify areas for improvement and refine your strategy.

Example: Company XYZ tracks metrics such as engagement rates, conversion rates, and deal close rates for accounts within each intent segment. By analyzing these metrics, the marketing and sales teams can gauge the effectiveness of their personalized approaches.

Remember, implementing intent data in an account-based marketing program involves a combination of technology, strategy, and creativity. By leveraging intent insights, companies can deliver more personalized and targeted experiences to their high-value accounts, ultimately increasing the likelihood of conversion and building long-term relationships.

CHAPTER 17

BEHAVIORAL DATA AND HOW TO LEVERAGE IN ACCOUNT-BASED MARKETING

Behavioral data plays a pivotal role in modern marketing strategies, particularly in the context of Account-Based Marketing (ABM). In this chapter, we'll delve into the concept of behavioral data, exploring what it is, how it is collected, and its significance in ABM. Additionally, we will give three examples illustrating the practical applications of behavioral data in creating and executing ABM campaigns.

Behavioral data refers to information that reveals how individuals or entities act, engage, and interact in digital spaces or, more specifically, online. As individuals are navigating public websites, data is being captured behind the scenes as it relates to this, like which web page you visited, how long you stayed on the site, which content you viewed, and the date and time of the website visit. All this information is valuable to marketers who are trying to identify individuals who are most likely to engage with their content and show a pattern or behavior that is favorable to the brand. In a marketing context, behavioral data provides insights into the online activities of prospects and customers, shedding light on their preferences, interests, and the various touchpoints they engage with throughout the customer journey. This data is collected from multiple sources, including websites, social media platforms, email interactions, and other online channels.

Types of Behavioral Data: Behavioral data can be broadly categorized into explicit and implicit types.

- Explicit Behavioral Data: This type of data is intentionally provided by individuals. It includes actions such as form submissions, survey responses, and explicit preferences expressed by users.
- Implicit Behavioral Data: Implicit data is collected passively based on user actions and interactions. This includes website visits, content consumption, click-through rates, and other digital footprints that users leave behind.

Behavioral Data can vary, and several tools and technologies are employed to collect behavioral data:

- Website Analytics: Tools like Google Analytics track user interactions on websites, providing insights into page views, click paths, and time spent on different pages.
- Marketing Automation Platforms: Platforms like HubSpot or Marketo capture behavioral data related to email interactions, form submissions, and engagement with marketing campaigns.
- Customer Relationship Management (CRM) Systems: CRM systems store data on customer interactions and transactions, offering a comprehensive view of the customer's journey.

- Social Media Monitoring Tools: Tools like Hootsuite or Brandwatch track social media engagement, including likes, shares, and comments, providing valuable insights into audience behavior on social platforms.

The Significance of Behavioral Data in Account-Based Marketing

In the context of ABM, understanding and leveraging behavioral data is essential for creating highly personalized and targeted campaigns. ABM focuses on treating individual accounts as markets of one, and behavioral data plays a crucial role in tailoring interactions to the specific needs and interests of each target account. Here are three examples of how behavioral data can be used in ABM:

1. Personalization of Content and Messaging:

Behavioral data allows marketers to create highly personalized content and messaging strategies. By analyzing how target accounts interact with content, websites, and other marketing materials, it becomes possible to tailor messages to align with the specific interests and preferences of each account.

Example: Consider a software company engaged in ABM. Behavioral data reveals that a particular target account has been consistently engaging with content related to cybersecurity solutions. In response, the marketing team can create personalized content highlighting the security features of their software, addressing the specific concerns of that account.

2. Lead Scoring and Prioritization:

Behavioral data is instrumental in lead scoring within ABM. By assigning scores based on the intensity of engagement and the types of interactions exhibited by target accounts, marketing, and sales teams can prioritize their efforts on accounts that display higher levels of interest and are more likely to convert.

Example: In an ABM campaign, behavioral data indicates that a key decision-maker within a target account has attended multiple webinars, downloaded case studies, and visited pricing pages. This high level of engagement prompts the sales team to prioritize this account for personalized outreach, recognizing the strong indication of purchase intent.

3. Triggering Automated Campaigns:

Behavioral data can be used to trigger automated campaigns and workflows. When certain predefined behaviors are detected, automated responses such as personalized emails, targeted ads, or follow-up content can be deployed, ensuring a timely and relevant approach.

Example: Imagine an e-commerce company using ABM. Behavioral data shows that a target account has repeatedly visited specific product pages and added items to their cart but hasn't completed the purchase. An automated email campaign can be triggered, offering a discount or additional information to encourage the account to finalize the purchase.

While behavioral data is a powerful tool in ABM, there are challenges and considerations to keep in mind:

- Privacy Concerns: With increasing emphasis on data privacy, it's crucial to handle behavioral data ethically and in compliance with regulations such as GDPR. Obtaining explicit consent for data collection and ensuring secure storage and processing are essential.
- Data Accuracy: The accuracy of behavioral data is paramount. Inaccurate or outdated information can lead to misguided marketing efforts. Regularly validate and update behavioral data to maintain its reliability.
- Integration of Data Sources: ABM campaigns often involve multiple tools and platforms. Ensuring seamless integration between these systems is essential for a cohesive and holistic view of behavioral data.
- Interpreting Complex Data Sets: Behavioral data can be complex, encompassing a wide range of interactions. Marketers must have the tools and expertise to interpret these data sets effectively and derive actionable insights.

In the landscape of modern marketing, behavioral data stands out as a valuable asset, especially within the context of Account-Based Marketing. By leveraging the insights derived from the online actions of target accounts, marketers can craft highly personalized and targeted campaigns. Whether it's tailoring content, prioritizing leads, or triggering automated responses, behavioral data plays a central role in optimizing the ABM approach. However, it's crucial to navigate challenges related to privacy, data accuracy, and integration to fully harness the potential of behavioral data in driving successful ABM campaigns.

CHAPTER 18

ACCOUNT-BASED MARKETING METRICS AND ANALYTICS

Digital metrics and analytics play a pivotal role in modern marketing strategies, providing a wealth of data that enables marketers to assess performance, refine strategies, and enhance overall effectiveness.

Account-Based Marketing (ABM) metrics are essential for measuring the effectiveness of your ABM strategies and campaigns. These metrics help you track the progress of your efforts, understand the impact on target accounts, and make data-driven decisions to optimize your marketing and sales tactics. Below, I'll provide examples of specific ABM metrics in detail:

1. **Target Account Engagement Metric and Account Engagement Score:**

The Account Engagement Score is a composite metric that quantifies how actively your target accounts are interacting with your content and campaigns. It combines various engagement signals, such as website visits, email opens, click-through rates, and social media interactions.

Example: An account engagement score of 85 indicates that the target account is highly engaged with your content and campaigns, suggesting a higher likelihood of conversion.

2. Pipeline Contribution Metric:

Pipeline Generated measures the total dollar value of opportunities created as a result of your ABM efforts. It quantifies the contribution of ABM campaigns to the sales pipeline.

Example: If your ABM efforts have generated $500,000 in potential opportunities, that is the value you would report for this metric.

3. Account Conversion Rate Metric:

Account Conversion Rate calculates the percentage of target accounts that have moved from one stage of the sales funnel to the next. It shows how effectively your ABM strategies are moving accounts towards conversion.

Example: If 15 out of 100 target accounts moved from the "Awareness" stage to the "Consideration" stage, the account conversion rate would be 15%.

4. Account-Wide Revenue Metric:

Account Revenue measures the total revenue generated from a specific target account, including all deals and cross-sell or upsell opportunities. It provides a comprehensive view of the account's value.

Example: If a target account has generated $100,000 in revenue from initial deals and an additional $50,000 through upsell opportunities, the total account revenue would be $150,000.

5. Customer Acquisition Cost (CAC) Metric:

Customer Acquisition Cost calculates the average cost of acquiring a new customer from a target account. It includes expenses related to ABM campaigns and sales efforts.

Example: If your ABM campaign costs $10,000, and it successfully acquires five customers from the target account, the account CAC is $2,000.

6. Account Velocity Score:

Account Velocity measures the speed at which target accounts move through the sales funnel. It factors in the time it takes for an account to progress from initial engagement to conversion.

Example: An account with a high-velocity score indicates that it is quickly progressing through the sales funnel, while a low score suggests a longer conversion timeline.

7. Account Retention Rate:

Account Retention Rate calculates the percentage of target accounts that have continued to do business with your company over a specified period. It measures the effectiveness of retaining and growing relationships with target accounts.

Example: If you started with 50 target accounts, and 45 of them are still active after a year, the account retention rate is 90%.

8. Marketing Influence on Opportunities Metric:

Marketing-influenced opportunities quantify the number and value of opportunities that marketing has directly influenced through ABM campaigns and activities.

Example: If marketing influenced the creation of 20 opportunities with a total value of $200,000, that would be the metric reported.

9. Metric: Account Sales Cycle Length

Account Sales Cycle Length measures the average time it takes for a target account to move from initial engagement to conversion. It helps evaluate the efficiency of the sales process.

Example: If, on average, it takes 90 days for a target account to convert, the account sales cycle length is 90 days.

10. Customer Lifetime Value (CLV) Metric:

Account CLV calculates the total expected value of a customer from a specific target account over the course of the relationship. It considers initial purchases and potential future transactions.

Example: If the expected CLV for a target account is $50,000, that is the account CLV.

11. Account-Based ROI (ABM ROI) Metric:

ABM ROI measures the return on investment for your ABM campaigns. It compares the revenue generated from target accounts to the total costs associated with ABM efforts.

Example: If your ABM campaign generated $300,000 in revenue and the campaign cost $50,000, the ABM ROI would be 500% ($300,000 / $50,000).

12. Account Expansion Rate and Metric:

Account Expansion Rate tracks the percentage growth in revenue from a target account over a specific period. It reflects the success of upsell and cross-sell strategies.

Example: If a target account initially brought in $100,000 in revenue and, after an ABM campaign, the revenue increased to $120,000, the account expansion rate is 20%.

13. Account Churn Rate Metric:

Account Churn Rate measures the percentage of target accounts that stopped doing business with your company. It helps assess the health of customer relationships.

Example: If you started with 100 target accounts and lost 10 of them, the account churn rate is 10%.

Establish a cycle of analysis, optimization, and learning to refine marketing strategies continuously. Consider creating a weekly or monthly dashboard that you can report and provide you the insights to make better and informed decisions:

- Regular Reporting and Analysis: Conducting routine analysis of various metrics to identify trends and opportunities.
- Benchmarking and Goal Setting: Setting achievable benchmarks based on historical data and industry standards.
- Staying Agile: Adapting strategies based on real-time analytics to respond to changing market dynamics.

- Learning from Failures: Analyzing unsuccessful campaigns to understand what went wrong and avoid similar mistakes.
- Staying Updated: Keeping abreast of new analytics tools and methodologies to refine strategies continually.

These ABM metrics provide a comprehensive view of the performance and impact of your account-based marketing efforts. By tracking and analyzing these metrics, you can refine your ABM strategies, optimize resource allocation, and demonstrate the value of ABM to your organization.

CHAPTER 19

MAKING ACCOUNT-BASED MARKETING A COMPETITIVE ADVANTAGE

in the B2B marketing landscape by offering a unique approach to engaging high-value target accounts. ABM gives you the ability to focus on individual accounts as markets of one, tailoring messaging, content, and outreach to the specific needs and challenges of each account. Additionally, the level of insights across the different campaigns enables you to know which personnel in what organization is actively looking for your solution. This personalized and targeted approach delivers a multitude of competitive advantages for B2B businesses. In this chapter, we will explore the key benefits of implementing ABM and how it provides a substantial edge in the competitive B2B environment.

Let's look and remind ourselves of five key benefits of ABM:

1. Precision Targeting and Concentrated Resources

One of the primary advantages of ABM is precision targeting. Instead of casting a wide net to capture as many leads as possible, ABM enables B2B businesses to identify and focus on high-value accounts that are most likely to convert. By aligning sales and marketing efforts, organizations can concentrate their resources on these accounts. This ensures that time, budget, and personnel are allocated efficiently, resulting in a higher return on investment (ROI).

Example: An enterprise software company specializes in providing project management solutions to large construction firms. By implementing ABM, they identify specific Fortune 500 construction companies as their ideal customers. Instead of spreading their resources thinly, they concentrate their marketing and sales efforts on these high-value accounts. The result is a significantly higher ROI, as the majority of their revenue comes from these key accounts.

2. Personalization and Relevance

ABM places a strong emphasis on personalization and relevance. It enables businesses to create tailored messaging and content that directly address the unique needs and challenges of individual target accounts. By demonstrating a deep understanding of an account's specific situation, ABM builds trust and credibility. Personalization not only increases engagement but also improves conversion rates, as decision-makers are more likely to take action when they perceive that the content and solutions resonate with their specific concerns.

Example: A marketing agency implements ABM to target a group of financial institutions. They create customized content that addresses the specific challenges faced by each institution, such as regulatory compliance and risk management. This personalized approach results in higher engagement and conversion rates.

3. Improved Lead Quality

ABM's emphasis on precise targeting and personalization leads to improved lead quality. This means that the leads generated and engaged with are more likely to convert into valuable customers. High-quality leads closely match the ideal customer profile and are a good fit for the offerings, resulting in higher conversion rates. In addition, these leads often have shorter sales cycles, as they are already well-aligned with the business and require less time for education and decision-making.

Example: An IT services company targets mid-sized businesses. By precisely targeting accounts in need of IT support and personalizing their outreach with tailored solutions, they generate high-quality leads that have shorter sales cycles and a higher customer lifetime value.

4. Cost Efficiency

ABM's resource-efficient approach not only concentrates resources but also minimizes wastage. With precise targeting, businesses avoid marketing to accounts that are not a good fit for their offering. This prevents the allocation of resources to unqualified leads or accounts that are unlikely to convert. In addition, ABM's efficiency can lead to cost savings as organizations use their budget and personnel more effectively.

Example: A cybersecurity company focuses on precise targeting by identifying accounts in highly regulated industries like healthcare and finance. By concentrating on these specific accounts, they use their budget and resources more efficiently and avoid wasting resources on less relevant leads.

5. Stronger Customer Relationships

ABM fosters stronger customer relationships. By providing tailored solutions and demonstrating a deep understanding of an account's needs, organizations build trust and credibility. These relationships are essential in the B2B sales process, where decisions often involve significant investments and long-term commitments. Strong customer relationships lead to customer loyalty, repeat business, and potential word-of-mouth referrals.

Example: A software company targeting Fortune 500 companies in the manufacturing sector implements ABM. They focus their marketing and sales efforts on these high-value accounts, resulting in stronger relationships and long-term partnerships. These key accounts not only make repeat purchases but also refer the company to other potential clients.

ABM will create a substantial competitive advantage for your organization. Here are some areas for you to consider:

Focused Resource Allocation: ABM's precision targeting allows organizations to allocate resources more effectively. Instead of spreading their budget and personnel thin, they concentrate their efforts on the highest-potential accounts. This focused resource allocation results in a higher ROI, as marketing and sales teams are more likely to engage with the accounts most likely to convert.

Competitive Advantage: By efficiently utilizing their resources, businesses gain a financial edge over competitors who may not have such a targeted approach. They can achieve better results with the same budget or allocate fewer resources to achieve the same outcome.

Tailored Solutions: Personalization and relevance are key drivers of customer engagement and conversion. ABM enables organizations to tailor their messaging and content to address the specific needs and challenges of individual accounts. By providing solutions that are directly aligned with an account's situation, businesses position themselves as trusted advisors, which can be a significant competitive advantage.

Competitive Advantage: B2B businesses that offer tailored solutions through ABM gain a competitive edge. Their offerings are perceived as more valuable and relevant, increasing the likelihood of conversion compared to generic messaging.

Higher Conversion Rates: Improved lead quality, a direct result of ABM's precise targeting and personalization, leads to higher conversion rates. High-quality leads are more likely to convert into valuable customers, resulting in a better ROI. Shorter sales cycles, another outcome of ABM, further contribute to higher conversion rates, as high-quality leads require less time for education and decision-making.

Competitive Advantage: Organizations using ABM to achieve higher conversion rates outperform competitors who rely on less targeted approaches. They can close deals more efficiently and effectively.

Cost Efficiency: ABM's efficient resource allocation and minimized wastage result in cost efficiency. By avoiding marketing to unqualified leads and allocating resources only to high-value accounts, businesses reduce costs. The resource efficiency gained through ABM can lead to substantial cost savings in the long run.

Competitive Advantage: B2B organizations that leverage ABM's cost efficiency gain a competitive advantage by optimizing their budgets and maximizing their return on investment. This cost-saving approach allows them to allocate resources to other strategic initiatives.

Strong Customer Relationships: The relationships fostered through ABM are invaluable in B2B industries with lengthy sales cycles. Strong customer relationships are built on trust and credibility, and they can have a significant impact on customer loyalty and long-term partnerships. Satisfied customers are more likely to make repeat purchases and refer the business to others.

Companies that use ABM to build stronger customer relationships have a competitive advantage. Their customers are more likely to remain loyal and provide referrals, which can result in a continuous stream of business opportunities.

CHAPTER 20

THE SIGNIFICANCE OF BUYER PERSONAS IN B2B MARKETING

Creating buyer personas is a crucial component of any B2B marketing strategy. Personas are semi-fictional representations of your ideal customers, based on research and data about your existing customers and target audience. They help businesses understand their customers better, tailor their marketing efforts, and align their messaging and products with the specific needs and preferences of different customer segments. In this chapter, we'll explore the importance of creating personas in B2B marketing and provide detailed examples of four different B2B buyer personas.

Targeted Messaging: B2B marketing is all about communicating value to other businesses. By creating detailed buyer personas, you can tailor your messaging to speak directly to the pain points, goals, and preferences of each segment. This ensures that your marketing efforts are highly relevant and resonate with your audience.

Efficient Resource Allocation: Marketing resources, including time and budget, are often limited. By knowing who your ideal customers are, you can allocate your resources more efficiently, concentrating your efforts on the segments most likely to convert.

Improved Product Development: Buyer personas can provide insights into the specific needs and desires of your customers. This information can guide product development efforts, helping you create products and services that better meet your customers' requirements.

Enhanced Customer Retention: Understanding your customers' challenges and goals allows you to provide better ongoing support and services. This can lead to higher customer satisfaction and loyalty.

Better Lead Generation: When you know the characteristics of your ideal customers, you can design lead generation strategies that attract prospects with similar attributes, improving the quality of your leads.

The process of creating B2B buyer personas begins with describing the B2B buyer in detail. This means building a profile of an individual by giving them a name, age, gender, likes and dislikes, how they make decisions, and what they are responsible for in the organization. And it begins with gathering market data and research.

1. Gather Data:

Start by collecting data on your existing customers and target audience. This includes demographic information, job titles, industry, company size, and location. It's essential to gather information on their challenges, goals, pain points, and preferences.

2. Conduct Interviews:

To gather more in-depth insights, conduct interviews with customers and prospects. Ask questions about their buying process, decision-making criteria, and what influences their choices.

3. Analyze Data:

Review and analyze the data you've collected to identify patterns and common characteristics. Look for trends and shared pain points that can help you create segments.

4. Create Personas:

Based on the information you've gathered, start creating your buyer personas. Each persona should have a name, a detailed description, and specific attributes.

5. Validate and Refine:

Test your personas by using them in your marketing efforts. As you gain more data and experience, refine your personas to make them even more accurate.

Now, let's look at a few detailed examples of four B2B buyer personas:

Persona 1: IT Director

- Name: Dave Richardson
- Job Title: IT Director
- Company: Medium-sized technology company
- Industry: Information Technology

Business Challenges:

- Keeping the company's IT infrastructure secure from cyber threats
- Managing the IT budget and resources effectively
- Ensuring that all software and systems are up to date and functioning optimally

Business Goals:

- Improve the company's cybersecurity measures to protect sensitive data
- Optimize the IT infrastructure for better performance and reliability
- Find cost-effective solutions to reduce IT spending

Preferred Communication Channels:

- Dave prefers email and LinkedIn for professional communication.
- He occasionally attends industry conferences and webinars.

Decision-Making Process:

- Dave is typically involved in the early stages of the decision-making process.
- He consults with his IT team, C-suite, and finance department before making purchasing decisions.
- Peer recommendations and industry reports influence his choices.

Key Business Pain Points:

- Balancing security with accessibility for employees.
- Managing the IT team's workload efficiently.
- Ensuring compliance with industry regulations.

How to Engage Dave:

- Provide in-depth whitepapers and case studies on cybersecurity.
- Offer cost-effective solutions and potential ROI analyses.
- Showcase your products' ease of integration with existing systems.

Persona 2: Marketing Manager Melissa

- Name: Melissa Andrews
- Job Title: Marketing Manager
- Company: B2B SaaS startup
- Industry: Software and Technology

Key Business Challenges:

- Generating high-quality leads for the sales team.
- Proving ROI for marketing efforts.
- Keeping up with the latest digital marketing trends.

Key Business Goals:

- Increase lead generation and conversion rates.
- Demonstrate the impact of marketing campaigns on revenue.

- Stay ahead of competitors by implementing innovative marketing strategies.

Preferred Communication Channels:

- Melissa frequently uses email, LinkedIn, and Twitter for professional networking.
- She follows industry blogs, podcasts, and webinars to stay informed.

Decision-Making Process:

- Melissa often initiates the search for new marketing tools and strategies.
- She collaborates with the sales team, analyzes data, and reports to the company's leadership.

Key Business Pain Points:

- Lack of time and resources for comprehensive marketing strategies.
- Difficulty in finding marketing technology that aligns with the company's needs.
- Measuring the ROI of marketing campaigns.

How to Engage Melissa:

- Offer marketing automation solutions that save time and boost ROI.
- Provide case studies demonstrating how your product increased lead generation.
- Share content on the latest marketing trends and best practices.

Persona 3: Procurement Officer Sarah

Name: Sarah Mitchell

Job Title: Procurement Officer

Company: Large manufacturing corporation

Industry: Manufacturing

Key Business Challenges:

- Sourcing raw materials at competitive prices.
- Ensuring a stable and reliable supply chain.
- Managing supplier relationships and contracts.

Key Business Goals:

- Reduce procurement costs while maintaining product quality.
- Establish long-term relationships with reliable suppliers.
- Ensure a consistent supply of materials to support production.

Preferred Communication Channels:

- Sarah prefers email and phone calls for business communication.
- She occasionally attends industry-specific trade shows and conferences.

Decision-Making Process:

- Sarah plays a central role in supplier selection and contract negotiations.

- She collaborates with the finance and production departments to make informed decisions.

Key Business Pain Points:

- Balancing cost-cutting with quality assurance.
- Navigating complex supplier contracts and negotiations.
- Ensuring a smooth supply chain to prevent production delays.

How to Engage Sarah:

- Offer competitive pricing and long-term contract options.
- Highlight your commitment to quality control and reliable supply.
- Provide a straightforward and transparent contract negotiation process.

Persona 4: HR Manager Alex

Name: Alex Thompson

Job Title: HR Manager

Company: Mid-sized consulting firm

Industry: Professional Services

Key Business Challenges:

- Attracting and retaining top talent in a competitive job market.
- Ensuring compliance with labor laws and regulations.

- Managing employee performance and professional development.

Key Business Goals:

- Implement strategies to recruit and retain top talent.
- Stay compliant with evolving labor laws and regulations.
- Foster a positive and productive work environment.

Preferred Communication Channels:

- Alex prefers email and attends HR-related webinars and conferences.
- Professional social networks and HR industry publications are her primary sources of information.

Decision-Making Process:

- Alex is often involved in HR-related software and service purchasing decisions.
- She collaborates with the leadership team and legal counsel to ensure compliance.

Key Business Pain Points:

- Finding cost-effective solutions to streamline HR processes.
- Navigating complex legal requirements and compliance issues.
- Addressing employee relations and performance management challenges.

How to Engage Alex:

- Provide HR software solutions that simplify compliance and improve talent management.
- Offer resources on HR best practices, employee engagement, and compliance.
- Showcase case studies of companies that improved their HR processes using your solutions.

In summary, B2B buyer personas are valuable tools for tailoring your marketing strategies to meet the specific needs and preferences of different segments of your audience. By understanding the challenges, goals, and decision-making processes of individuals like IT Director Dave, Marketing Manager Melissa, Procurement Officer Sarah, and HR Manager Alex, you can create more effective marketing campaigns that resonate with your ideal customers, ultimately leading to increased engagement and conversions in your B2B marketing efforts.

CHAPTER 21

TECH STACK FOR YOUR ACCOUNT-BASED MARKETING PROGRAM

A tech stack in B2B marketing refers to the collection of software, tools, and technologies that businesses use to streamline, automate, and optimize their marketing efforts. It's a combination of various digital solutions designed to manage and enhance different facets of marketing activities in a business-to-business context. A well-constructed tech stack is integral to modern B2B marketing strategies due to its ability to improve efficiency, enable data-driven decisions, enhance customer experiences, and drive overall business growth.

Creating a comprehensive description of today's tech stack for Account-Based Marketing (ABM) in B2B tech companies requires an in-depth understanding of the technologies, tools, and strategies that have evolved to support this specialized marketing approach. ABM is a strategy where B2B tech companies focus their marketing efforts on a select group of high-value target accounts, tailoring their messaging and content to the specific needs and interests of each account. In this chapter, I will provide a detailed overview of the essential components of a modern ABM tech stack, including specific examples where relevant.

Data and Analytics will be key as well as a central database to store and track it:

A robust ABM tech stack begins with data and analytics to identify and prioritize target accounts effectively. It includes a Customer Relationship Management (CRM) System:

Examples: Salesforce, HubSpot, and Microsoft Dynamics

CRM systems are essential for managing and tracking interactions with target accounts. They provide a central database for storing account information, enabling sales and marketing teams to coordinate their efforts.

You will need a tool to help with Account Scoring and Prioritization:

These platforms use predictive analytics and machine learning to score and prioritize target accounts based on factors like firmographics, behavioral data, and engagement signals.

Examples: Demandbase, 6sense, and Engagio

Secure external third-party data to enhance your database like Intent Data Platforms: Intent data platforms monitor the online behavior of target accounts to identify signals of interest. This data helps marketers understand when an account is in a buying mindset.

Example: Bombora, G2, and TechTarget

The Tech stack will need tools to help you to capture tracking and analytics for reporting: Analytics tools help track the performance of ABM campaigns, measuring key metrics like engagement, conversion rates, and ROI.

Examples: Google Analytics, Adobe Analytics, and Tableau

Library of marketing content and personalization: ABM relies heavily on personalized content to engage target accounts effectively. This is your ebooks, whitepapers, case studies, blogs, etc. A CMS is essential for creating, managing, and delivering personalized content to target accounts. You will need to invest in a Content Management System (CMS):

Examples: WordPress, Drupal, and Sitecore

In order to have relevant and timely content, you should invest in Dynamic Content Personalization: These tools allow for real-time content personalization based on the behavior and preferences of the account's contacts.

Examples: Uberflip, PathFactory, and Adobe Target

Account-Based Messaging and Chatbots:

Chatbots and messaging platforms enable real-time conversations with target accounts, providing personalized responses and collecting valuable data.

Examples: Drift, Intercom, and Conversica

Email Marketing Tools: Email Marketing platforms support personalized email campaigns tailored to individual accounts.

Examples: Marketo, Pardot, and Mailchimp

Social Media Management: Social Media Management tools help schedule and analyze social posts targeting specific accounts.

Examples: Hootsuite, Sprout Social, and Buffer

Advertising and Retargeting: ABM often involves highly targeted advertising campaigns across various platforms.

Examples: Google Ads, LinkedIn Ads, and Terminus

Direct Mail Automation: Sending personalized physical gifts or direct mail pieces can be a powerful way to engage key accounts.

Examples: Sendoso, PFL, and Postalytics

Website Personalization tools: Web personalization tools deliver a customized experience when target accounts visit the company's website.

Examples: Evergage, Monetate, and Dynamic Yield

Sales and Marketing Alignment: Seamless coordination between sales and marketing teams is vital in ABM.

Sales Enablement Platforms: These platforms provide sales teams with the content, insights, and tools they need to engage target accounts effectively.

Examples: Seismic, Highspot, and Showpad

Marketing Automation: Marketing automation tools help create, manage, and analyze marketing campaigns, ensuring alignment with sales goals.

Examples: Marketo, Eloqua, and HubSpot

CRM Integration: Integration between CRM and marketing automation tools ensures smooth data flow and a unified view of account interactions.

Examples: Salesforce CRM integration with Pardot or HubSpot

Predictive Analytics and AI: Predictive analytics platforms help identify potential target accounts by analyzing data from various sources. Advanced technologies like AI and predictive analytics enhance ABM efforts.

Examples: InsideView, Mintigo, and Lattice Engines

AI-Powered Chatbots and Assistants: AI-driven chatbots and assistants can engage target accounts intelligently and automate conversations.

Examples: Conversica, Drift, and Intercom

Reporting and Attribution: Measuring and attributing results accurately is crucial for optimizing ABM efforts. These tools help determine the impact of different touchpoints on an account's journey.

Examples: Bizible, Full Circle Insights, and Adobe Analytics

Reporting Dashboards: Reporting dashboards provide a clear view of ABM performance, facilitating data-driven decision-making.

Examples: Tableau, Power BI, and Google Data Studio

Compliance and Data Security: In an era of increased data regulation, compliance and data security are paramount.

Data Privacy and Compliance Tools: These tools help B2B tech companies ensure that their ABM practices adhere to data protection regulations like GDPR and CCPA.

Examples: OneTrust, TrustArc, and Trustwave

Integration and Orchestration: Seamless integration between different tools is essential for a cohesive ABM tech stack. Integration platforms allow for the automation of workflows between various ABM tools.

Examples: Zapier, Integromat, and Workato

Account-Based Reporting and Analytics: Specialized reporting tools help measure the success of ABM campaigns.

Account-Based Reporting Tools may include Demandbase ABM Platform, Terminus, and Engagio. These tools offer specific reporting and analytics tailored to the unique needs of ABM programs.

Account-Based Sales Development (ABSD): ABSD tools support the sales development team in identifying, engaging, and converting target accounts. These platforms help sales development representatives manage and automate their outreach efforts to target accounts.

Examples: Outreach, SalesLoft, and Groove

Account Intelligence: Account intelligence tools provide detailed information about target accounts to assist sales reps in crafting personalized outreach.

Examples: DiscoverOrg, ZoomInfo, and LinkedIn Sales Navigator

Mobile Marketing and Engagement Tools: These tools enable personalized mobile engagement with target accounts through apps and SMS. Mobile engagement is increasingly important in the B2B space.

Examples: Leanplum, Localytics, and Airship

Customer Data Platforms (CDP): CDPs play a role in unifying and activating customer data for ABM. CDPs help collect, unify, and activate customer data which can be valuable for creating personalized ABM experiences.

Examples: Segment, Tealium, and BlueConic

Conversational AI: Conversational AI can power chatbots and virtual assistants to engage target accounts through natural language interactions.

Examples: Ada, Yellow Messenger, and Conversica

Customer Advocacy and Referral Programs: Leveraging customer advocates in ABM can be highly effective. These platforms help B2B tech companies identify and engage their customers as advocates who can influence target accounts.

Examples: Influitive, G2 Advocate Hub, and Ambassador

Competitive Intelligence: Understanding the competitive landscape is crucial for ABM's success. These platforms provide insights into competitors' strategies and help shape an effective ABM plan.

Examples: Crayon, Kompyte, and Klue

The modern tech stack for Account-Based Marketing in B2B tech companies is a complex and evolving ecosystem of tools and technologies designed to identify, engage, and convert high-value target accounts. The key is to start slow and with just a few of the tools and integrate them successfully.

Start with a CRM, marketing automation tool, content management system, analytics, and reporting engine. And build from there.

The tech stack outlined in this chapter encompasses data and analytics, content and personalization, account engagement, sales and marketing alignment, predictive analytics, compliance and data security, integration and orchestration, and many other components. As technology continues to advance, the ABM tech stack will likely expand to include emerging technologies, further enhancing the ability to engage and convert target accounts effectively.

CHAPTER 22

ACCOUNT BASED MARKETING REQUIRES A SPECIALIZED TEAM

Implementing a successful Account-Based Marketing (ABM) approach requires a specialized team with a unique skill set and a deep understanding of the target accounts. The typical marketing staffing for ABM consists of various roles and responsibilities, each contributing to different aspects of the ABM strategy. In this chapter, I'll describe in detail the key roles and their responsibilities so that you can utilize them to build your ABM team:

- **Account-Based Marketing Strategist:**
  Develops and oversees the overall ABM strategy, including identifying target accounts, setting goals, and defining key tactics. This role will help to build personas, define the positioning, messaging, create use cases for your product and/or solution, and outline the entire go-to marketing plan. This role is also responsible for collaborating with sales and marketing teams to align strategies and objectives as well as monitor market trends and adjust the ABM strategy as needed. Moreover, they

define the customer journey for target accounts and create a personalized plan.

- **Account-Based Marketing Manager:**
  This role can at times be called a campaign manager. Their responsibility is to execute the ABM strategy and plan, ensuring campaigns are on track. They collaborate with cross-functional teams, such as content marketing, demand generation, and sales, to deliver account-specific content and experiences. They should be knowledgeable of the different ABM technology platforms and tools, ensuring they are optimized for account engagement. They also analyze campaign performance and provide regular reports on KPIs.

- **Data Analyst or Marketing Operations:**
  This role is responsible for the marketing technical stack. Building the marketing database, integrating all the different technologies and tools, and defining tracking methodology to collect and analyze data related to target accounts and their behavior. They identify trends and insights that can guide the ABM strategy. They ensure data quality and integrity for account segmentation. Collaborate with the ABM manager to refine target account lists.

Content Creator and Strategist:

This role's responsibilities are to create and curate account-specific content and assets tailored to target accounts. They develop a content plan that aligns with the account journey and messaging and collaborates with designers and writers to produce personalized content. They ensure consistency and alignment with the overall brand messaging.

Creative Team (Designers and Copywriters):

The creative team's responsibilities include producing visually appealing and compelling content, including emails, landing pages, and personalized assets. They work closely with the content strategist to create customized materials for target accounts to ensure brand consistency while tailoring content to individual accounts.

The above roles should be the core functions in your marketing department to successfully build the ABM program. As you continue to grow, additional roles and responsibilities will emerge that you will need. Initially, some of these roles could be freelancers but as the business revenues grow and the number of campaigns, content, and events that you need to support, it will make more sense to have direct hires.

Here are additional resources to consider as you grow the organization.

- **Demand Generation Specialist's** responsibilities are to create and execute demand generation campaigns that align with the ABM strategy. They leverage marketing automation tools for targeted account outreach and optimize paid advertising campaigns for target account engagement. They monitor and report on the effectiveness of demand-generation efforts.

- **Marketing Automation Specialist's** responsibilities include managing marketing automation platforms for personalized communication with target accounts. They set up and optimize email workflows, lead scoring, and tracking. Collaborate with the content strategist to ensure the right content is delivered at the right time. They monitor and troubleshoot technical issues related to automation.
- **Social Media Specialist's** responsibilities are to develop and execute social media strategies for engaging target accounts and monitor social platforms for account-specific conversations and engagement opportunities. They create and curate content for social channels that align with the ABM strategy. They also analyze social media data for insights into account behavior.
- **SEO/SEM Specialist** is responsible for optimizing online content and campaigns to ensure visibility among target accounts. They conduct keyword research and analysis specific to the target accounts and manage paid search campaigns to target account segments. They also monitor and report on SEO/SEM performance for target accounts.
- **Account-Based Advertising Manager** is responsible to plan and execute account-based advertising campaigns on platforms like LinkedIn, Google Ads, and other relevant channels. They are entrusted with optimizing ad targeting to reach target accounts effectively and

collaborate with the content strategist to create ad content that resonates with account-specific needs and pain points. They also track ad performance and adjust campaigns as needed.

- **Account Development Representatives (ADRs** are responsible for working closely with the sales team to engage and nurture target accounts, initiate outreach, and coordinate meetings with key decision-makers. They Provide valuable insights from account interactions to refine the ABM strategy.
- **Sales Alignment Manager** will be responsible for building a bridge between marketing and sales teams to ensure alignment and collaboration as well as define and communicate the roles and responsibilities of both teams in the ABM process. They also facilitate regular meetings and communication between marketing and sales teams to discuss account progress.
- **Project Manager** is responsible for ensuring that ABM campaigns and projects are executed on time and within budget. They coordinate efforts between different teams, manage project timelines, and identify and mitigate risks that may impact the success of ABM initiatives.

In summary, a successful ABM approach requires a dedicated team with a mix of skills and expertise, including strategy, data analysis, content creation, technical proficiency, and close collaboration with sales teams. The roles mentioned above play crucial parts in planning, executing, and optimizing ABM campaigns to effectively engage and convert high-value target accounts. The team's collective efforts are essential in delivering a personalized and impactful ABM experience for these accounts.

CHAPTER 23

ACCOUNT BASED MARKETING FOR YOUR MOBILE MARKETING PROGRAMS

Implementing Account-Based Marketing (ABM) for mobile marketing involves leveraging mobile-specific strategies and technologies to target and engage specific high-value accounts. Here's a step-by-step guide to implementing ABM for mobile marketing:

Identify Target Accounts and Segmentation:

Define your ideal customer profile (ICP) and identify high-value target accounts that align with your business objectives.

Segment these accounts based on industry, company size, demographics, behavior, and other relevant criteria.

Data Collection and Enrichment:

Gather comprehensive data about the target accounts, including contact information, preferences, past interactions, and challenges.

Enrich your data with mobile-specific insights, such as mobile usage patterns, app preferences, or mobile behavior data (if available).

Personalized Mobile Content and Messaging:

Create tailored and personalized mobile content for your target accounts. This could include mobile-optimized landing pages, interactive content, or mobile apps.

Craft messaging that resonates with the specific pain points, needs, and challenges of the target accounts.

Mobile Advertising and Targeting:

Use mobile advertising platforms to reach target accounts through precise targeting. Utilize geotargeting, device targeting, and specific app placements to reach the desired audience.

Leverage social media platforms that have robust mobile advertising capabilities for targeted account-based campaigns.

Mobile-Enabled Sales Engagement:

Equip your sales team with mobile tools and resources tailored for personalized interactions with target accounts.

Provide mobile-friendly sales collateral, demos, or presentations that align with the mobile preferences of the accounts.

6. Mobile-Specific Personalization and Engagement:

Implement mobile-specific personalization techniques such as in-app messages, push notifications, or SMS campaigns tailored to target accounts' preferences and behaviors.

Leverage mobile automation tools to deliver personalized content at optimal times based on mobile usage patterns.

Measurement and Analytics:

Implement mobile-specific analytics tools to track engagement, conversions, and interactions from target accounts across mobile channels.

Measure the effectiveness of your ABM mobile campaigns by analyzing metrics like app downloads, mobile site visits, or conversions attributed to mobile interactions.

Iterate and Optimize:

Continuously analyze data and insights to refine your mobile ABM strategy. Use A/B testing and performance analysis to optimize messaging, targeting, and content delivery.

Adapt your approach based on the feedback and engagement patterns received from target accounts.

Implementing ABM for mobile marketing involves a blend of data-driven targeting, personalized mobile content, and leveraging mobile-specific channels to engage and nurture relationships with high-value accounts. By aligning mobile strategies with the specific needs and preferences of targeted accounts, organizations can effectively drive engagement and conversions within their most valuable audience segments.

Five Detail Examples of how to Implement ABM in Your Mobile Marketing

Implementing Account-Based Marketing (ABM) with a focus on mobile marketing involves tailoring strategies to engage specific high-value accounts through mobile channels. Here are five detailed examples of how to implement ABM with mobile marketing:

Mobile-Optimized Personalized Content:

Strategy: Develop personalized content specifically optimized for mobile devices to engage target accounts.

Implementation: Create mobile-responsive landing pages or microsites tailored to each targeted account. These pages should reflect the account's pain points, needs, and interests.

Design interactive and engaging content formats such as quizzes, calculators, or assessments optimized for mobile viewing.

Example: A software company targets a high-value account in the healthcare industry. They create a mobile-optimized interactive calculator demonstrating potential cost savings from using their software, accessible via a personalized landing page.

Precision Targeting Through Mobile Advertising:

Strategy: Utilize mobile advertising platforms to reach target accounts with precision targeting.

Implementation: Employ geotargeting, device targeting, or mobile app targeting to deliver ads directly to the target accounts' mobile devices.

Craft tailored ad content that speaks directly to the pain points and solutions relevant to the targeted accounts.

Example: An enterprise SaaS company runs mobile ads targeted specifically at decision-makers within the selected accounts, promoting a webinar addressing challenges unique to their industry.

Personalized Mobile Messaging and Outreach:

Strategy: Engage target accounts through personalized mobile messaging channels.

Implementation: Implement personalized SMS campaigns or push notifications delivering targeted content or offers relevant to the account's needs.

Use mobile messaging apps or in-app messaging to initiate conversations or provide exclusive content tailored to individual accounts.

Example: A marketing agency sends personalized push notifications to key decision-makers within target accounts, offering a tailored e-book addressing their specific industry challenges.

Mobile-Friendly Sales Enablement:

Strategy: Equip sales teams with mobile tools to enhance interactions with target accounts.

Implementation: Provide sales reps with mobile-friendly presentations, product demos, or interactive tools accessible on tablets or smartphones.

Enable mobile-based CRM or sales automation tools that allow reps to engage with targeted accounts efficiently.

Example: A technology solutions provider equips its sales team with a mobile app containing personalized product demos and case studies for direct presentations during meetings with targeted accounts.

Mobile-Specific Engagement Tracking and Analytics:

Strategy: Implement mobile-specific analytics to track engagement and measure the success of ABM efforts.

Implementation: Use mobile analytics tools to track and analyze interactions, conversions, and engagement metrics specifically from mobile channels.

Generate reports focusing on mobile-specific metrics to assess the impact and ROI of ABM campaigns on mobile devices.

Example: A B2B software company uses mobile analytics to track the engagement levels of target accounts with their mobile-optimized landing pages, enabling them to optimize content based on mobile user behavior.

These examples demonstrate how to leverage mobile channels for personalized engagement, precise targeting, and tracking in an ABM strategy. By tailoring mobile marketing efforts to the specific needs and behaviors of high-value accounts, organizations can effectively drive engagement and conversions within their targeted audience segments.

CHAPTER 24

STEP-BY-STEP GUIDE TO IMPLEMENTING ABM FOR EMAIL MARKETING

Implementing Account-Based Marketing (ABM) within email marketing involves tailoring email strategies to target specific high-value accounts. Here's a step-by-step guide to implementing ABM for email marketing:

Identify and Segment Target Accounts:

Strategy: Define high-value target accounts aligned with your business goals.

Implementation: Identify accounts based on factors such as company size, industry, revenue potential, or strategic fit.

Segment these accounts into specific lists or groups based on common characteristics or needs.

Gather Account-Specific Data:

Strategy: Collect and enrich data about the target accounts.

Implementation: Gather account-specific information, including contacts, roles, preferences, challenges, and pain points.

Enrich your data with insights relevant to the targeted accounts' industries or segments.

Personalize Email Content for Target Accounts:

Strategy: Create tailored and personalized email content that resonates with target accounts.

Implementation: Craft customized email templates addressing the specific pain points or challenges of each account.

Personalize the email subject lines, content, and CTAs to align with the needs of individual accounts.

Targeted Email Campaigns:

Strategy: Run targeted email campaigns directed at specific accounts.

Implementation: Use segmentation to send personalized email sequences or nurture campaigns to targeted account lists.

Leverage dynamic content and personalization tokens to tailor email content based on account-specific data.

Account-Centric Email Outreach:

Strategy: Engage with targeted accounts through personalized outreach.

Implementation: Assign dedicated account managers or sales reps to handle email communications with targeted accounts.

Send personalized one-to-one emails addressing the account's specific challenges or offering tailored solutions.

Measure Account-Specific Metrics:

Strategy: Track and measure the performance of ABM email campaigns.

Implementation: Monitor email open rates, click-through rates, conversions, and responses from targeted accounts.

Use email analytics and tracking tools to assess the engagement and success of email interactions with targeted accounts.

Optimize and Iterate:

Strategy: Continuously optimize ABM email campaigns based on insights.

Implementation: Analyze performance metrics to identify areas for improvement and optimization.

Test different email elements (subject lines, content, CTAs) and iterate based on what resonates best with targeted accounts.

8. Align Email Marketing with Sales Efforts:

Strategy: Foster alignment between email marketing and sales efforts for targeted accounts.

Implementation: Ensure seamless communication between marketing and sales teams regarding account-specific interactions and responses.

Use email engagement data to inform and guide sales conversations with targeted accounts.

Implementing ABM for email marketing involves a strategic alignment of data, content, and outreach efforts tailored to specific high-value accounts. By delivering personalized and targeted email campaigns, organizations can effectively engage and nurture relationships with their most valuable prospects, driving higher conversions and fostering long-term partnerships.

To help you to get started, here are five detailed examples of emails used in Account-Based Marketing (ABM) strategies.

Personalized Introduction Email:

Objective: Introduce your company's value proposition to the targeted account.

Content: Subject Line: Address the account or industry directly for personalization (e.g., "Enhancing [Company's Name]'s Operations with [Your Solution]").

Body: Introduce yourself and your company, highlighting specific pain points or challenges the recipient's company might be facing. Offer a brief insight into how your solution addresses these challenges. Include case studies or success stories relevant to their industry.

CTA: Invite them to engage further, such as scheduling a call, attending a webinar, or exploring additional resources.

Case Study or Success Story Email:

Objective: Showcase successful implementations similar to the targeted account's industry or challenges.

Content: Subject Line: Highlight the success story or achievement (e.g., "How [Similar Company] Achieved [Specific Result] with [Your Solution]").

Body: Share a detailed case study or success story relevant to the target account's industry or pain points. Illustrate the challenges faced, the solutions provided, and the tangible results achieved. Emphasize how your solution can address similar challenges for them.

CTA: Encourage them to explore more success stories or schedule a demo to learn how it applies to their situation.

Solution Demo or Product Showcase Email:

Objective: Provide a detailed overview or demo of your solution tailored to the account's needs.

Content: Subject Line: Highlight the benefits of a solution demonstration (e.g., "See How [Your Solution] Can Transform [Account's Pain Point]").

Body: Offer a personalized and interactive demo or showcase of your product/service. Focus on features or functionalities that directly address the challenges or pain points identified for the targeted account. Use visuals, videos, or interactive elements to engage the recipient.

CTA: Encourage them to schedule a personalized demo or request more information based on their specific interests.

Thought Leadership Content Email:

Objective: Position your company as an industry thought leader and provide valuable insights.

Content: Subject Line: Highlight the value of the content (e.g., "New Insights on [Industry Trend/Challenge] from [Your Company]").

Body: Offer valuable content such as whitepapers, research reports, or industry insights addressing current trends, challenges, or opportunities relevant to the target account's industry. Show how your company is at the forefront of addressing these issues.

CTA: Encourage them to download the content or engage further with your resources.

Exclusive Offer or Customized Solution Email:

Objective: Present a tailored offer or solution specifically designed for the targeted account.

Content: Subject Line: Highlight exclusivity or customization (e.g., "Exclusive Offer: Tailored [Your Solution] for [Company's Name]").

Body: Propose a customized solution or offer exclusive benefits specifically tailored to the target account's needs. Address their pain points directly and outline how your solution can solve these challenges uniquely for them. Provide clear details of the offer, including any personalized pricing or package options.

CTA: Encourage them to discuss further, request a quote, or engage in a personalized consultation.

These email examples aim to deliver tailored and personalized content addressing the specific needs, pain points, and interests of targeted accounts. By providing valuable insights, demonstrating solutions, and offering customized approaches, these emails aim to engage and nurture relationships with high-value prospects in an Account-Based Marketing strategy.

CHAPTER 25

CUSTOMER RELATIONSHIP MANAGEMENT (CRM) SYSTEM CRUCIAL IN ACCOUNT-BASED MARKETING

So far in this book we have discussed all the major marketing programs and how to implement successful ABM programs for each. But we assumed that everyone understands that at the heart of a successful ABM program is a customer relationship management system. I have devoted this entire chapter to understanding the importance.

A Customer Relationship Management (CRM) system plays a pivotal role in the success of an Account-Based Marketing (ABM) strategy by serving as the central hub for managing, tracking, and nurturing relationships with targeted accounts. Here's why a CRM is crucial in ABM:

Centralized Data Management:

Account Insights: A CRM consolidates account-related data, including contacts, interactions, preferences, and buying behaviors, allowing a comprehensive view of each targeted account.

Historical Interactions: It records past communications, engagements, and touchpoints, providing valuable insights into previous interactions with targeted accounts.

Account Segmentation and Targeting:

Customized Segmentation: CRM allows the segmentation of accounts based on various criteria (industry, size, behavior), enabling targeted and personalized communication strategies for each account segment.

Focused Targeting: With CRM data, ABM efforts can be precisely targeted, ensuring that marketing and sales activities align with the unique needs of each account.

Coordination between Marketing and Sales:

Seamless Collaboration: A CRM fosters alignment between marketing and sales teams by providing shared access to account information, ensuring both teams work toward common goals.

Lead Handoff: It facilitates the smooth handoff of leads from marketing to sales, ensuring a cohesive and consistent approach in engaging targeted accounts.

Personalization and Customization:

Tailored Communication: CRM data allows for personalized and customized communication strategies, enabling marketers to craft messages, content, and offers specific to each account's needs and preferences.

Precise Targeting: By leveraging CRM insights, marketers can deliver highly targeted and relevant content, increasing the effectiveness of ABM campaigns.

Performance Measurement and Optimization:

Tracking and Analytics: A CRM provides tools to track the effectiveness of ABM campaigns, measuring engagement metrics, conversions, and ROI for each targeted account.

Continuous Improvement: Insights from CRM analytics help in refining strategies, optimizing campaigns, and allocating resources more effectively to drive better results.

Account-Based Reporting and Forecasting:

Account Visibility: CRM allows for dedicated reporting on the performance and progress of individual targeted accounts, enabling a clear understanding of the impact of ABM efforts.

Forecasting and Planning: It aids in forecasting revenue potential from targeted accounts, guiding future resource allocation and strategic planning.

Automation and Workflow Management:

Efficient Processes: CRM automation streamlines workflows, automating routine tasks, and enabling timely and targeted interactions with targeted accounts.

Scalability: Automation allows for scalability in managing multiple targeted accounts without compromising personalization and engagement quality.

In summary, a CRM system is indispensable in Account-Based Marketing as it empowers organizations to effectively manage relationships, personalize communication, collaborate between teams, measure performance, and drive successful engagements with high-value targeted accounts. The centralized data and streamlined processes provided by a CRM are instrumental in executing and optimizing an ABM strategy.

Conclusion

THE IMPERATIVE FOR B2B TECH COMPANIES TO EMBRACE ACCOUNT-BASED MARKETING IN 2024

I hope this book has been valuable to you and your search to not only understanding Account-Based marketing but how you can implement it successfully across your organization. The case for embracing Account-Based Marketing (ABM) has never been stronger. B2B tech companies are navigating an environment characterized by increased competition, evolving customer expectations, and rapidly advancing technology. To not just survive but thrive in this digital world that we are all part of, and we receive so much emails, text messages and social media requests to connect with little to no value. Account-Based Marketing will help you to build deeper engagement, distribute valuable content and generate more quality that leads to growth in your revenue and your business. In this conclusion, I will recap the key reasons why all B2B tech companies should consider implementing an ABM program and I extend my best wishes for the journey into this exciting marketing frontier.

Hyper-Personalization for Target Accounts:

The tech industry is known for its complexity, where decision-makers are often well-versed in the subject matter. ABM's personalized approach allows B2B tech companies to speak directly to the specific needs, challenges, and goals of each target account. By tailoring messaging and content to resonate with the individual nuances of an account, you can demonstrate a deep understanding of their situation. This level of hyper-personalization sets you apart in an industry where generic marketing often falls flat.

Precise Targeting in a Crowded Space:

The B2B tech landscape is crowded, with numerous companies vying for the attention of the same target audience. ABM's precise targeting enables you to cut through the noise by identifying high-value accounts that align with your ideal customer profile. Instead of employing a broad approach that risks spreading resources thin, you can concentrate your efforts on the accounts most likely to convert. This not only results in resource efficiency but also positions you as a thought leader in the eyes of key accounts.

Improved Lead Quality and Conversion Rates:

The tech industry thrives on innovation and efficiency, and ABM complements this ethos by delivering high-quality leads that are more likely to convert into valuable customers. By nurturing leads that closely match your ideal customer profile and are a good fit for your solutions, you'll experience higher conversion rates. Additionally, shorter sales cycles for high-quality leads mean you can accelerate your revenue generation, meeting the fast-paced demands of the tech sector.

Cost Efficiency and Resource Optimization:

Efficient resource allocation is a hallmark of ABM. In a time when budgets are scrutinized, ABM allows B2B tech companies to minimize wastage and avoid marketing to unqualified leads. By focusing on high-value accounts, you can allocate your budget and personnel with precision, making every marketing dollar count. The cost efficiency gained through ABM not only improves your return on investment but also enables you to direct resources toward strategic initiatives and innovations.

Stronger Customer Relationships and Long-Term Partnerships:

In an industry where technology solutions are long-term commitments and investments, strong customer relationships are paramount. ABM fosters these relationships by tailoring your outreach to align with the unique needs of each account. By building trust and credibility through tailored solutions and targeted engagement, you lay the foundation for enduring partnerships. Tech companies that implement ABM can cultivate loyal customers who are not only likely to make repeat purchases but also act as advocates for your solutions.

Best Wishes on Your ABM Journey:

As you embark on your journey into the world of Account-Based Marketing in 2024, we extend our warmest wishes for success.

The adoption of ABM is a transformative step that holds the promise of differentiating your B2B tech company in a highly competitive landscape. With personalization, precise targeting, improved lead quality, cost efficiency, and stronger customer relationships at your disposal, you are poised to take your marketing efforts to new heights.

Remember that the success of your ABM program lies in your ability to embrace the principles of data-driven decision-making, continuous adaptation, and the cultivation of a customer-centric culture. ABM is not a one-time endeavor but an ongoing commitment to nurturing meaningful relationships and delivering tailored solutions to your most valued accounts.

In the ever-evolving tech industry, where innovation is the driving force, ABM equips you with the tools to position your company as an industry leader. It allows you to speak directly to the needs of key decision-makers, paving the way for productive and long-lasting partnerships. Your journey into ABM is a testament to your commitment to providing exceptional value to your customers and driving innovation in the B2B tech sector.

So, as you navigate the exciting opportunities and challenges that await, may your ABM journey be marked by precision, personalization, and progress. May you build strong customer relationships that endure, create cost-efficient campaigns that yield impressive returns, and revel in the success of high-quality leads and conversions. In 2024, and beyond, may your B2B tech company shine brightly in the realm of Account-Based Marketing.

Wishing you all the best on this transformative journey into ABM. May your efforts be rewarded with growth, innovation, and lasting success.

ABOUT THE AUTHOR

Sebastian Pistritto, chief marketing officer with over 20 years of multichannel marketing communication, strategy, public relations, branding , and product management . He is experienced in industries such as technology, health care, retail, automotive, financial, software, and consumer electronics. He has also served as the Chief Marketing Officer for several organizations, responsible for marketing communications, brand management, and strategy. Sebastian is an experienced Enterprise Software Marketing Executive with 20 years of experience developing go-to-market strategies and brand narratives, building high-performance teams, and driving demand generation.

Over his career he has been responsible for the following:

- Develop and execute comprehensive marketing strategies to drive customer acquisition, retention, and engagement.
- Lead a team of marketing professionals, providing guidance, mentorship, and support to ensure the successful implementation of marketing plans.
- Use market research and analysis to identify trends, insights, and opportunities, and translate them into actionable marketing strategies.

- Collaborate with product management, sales, and other cross-functional teams to develop integrated marketing strategies and briefs that align with business objectives.
- Oversee the development and execution of multi-channel marketing campaigns, including digital marketing, social media, email marketing, content marketing, and traditional advertising.
- Drive brand awareness and recognition through effective messaging, storytelling, and creative campaigns.
- Partner with marketing leaders to monitor and analyze marketing campaign performance, track key performance indicators (KPIs), and make data-driven decisions to optimize marketing efforts and maximize ROI.
- Stay abreast of industry trends, emerging technologies, and best practices in consumer marketing to identify new opportunities for growth and innovation.
- Manage marketing budgets, allocate resources effectively, and ensure cost-effective marketing campaigns.

Pistritto has published numerous articles including *7 Steps on Engaging with Mobile Consumers*, **Selecting an Adserver Technology**, and *Managing Your Lead Qualification Process*, which have appeared in Internet.com, Mobile Marketer, MicroStation Manager Magazine, CtrlAltDelete Newsletter, VARiety Newsletter, InView Newsletter, and Insider Reports Journal. He is also a recipient of the 2000 Distinguished Technical Communication Award from the Society for Technical Communication.

Pistritto has presented at a number of industry events such as the Consumer Electronic Show (CES), Storage Visions-Home Network, Intel Developer Forum, CEATEC JAPAN, and Fall Focus: On-demand Digital Entertainment conference.

Pistritto brings marketing leadership experience and a proven track record of driving transformative growth. He holds a Bachelor of Science in Business Administration from Wilmington University and resides with his family in Pennsylvania.

APPENDIX

Digital metrics and analytics play a pivotal role in modern marketing strategies, providing a wealth of data that enables marketers to assess performance, refine strategies, and enhance overall effectiveness. In this section, I have outlined the extensive array of digital metrics available and explained what they are and how you can include them in your marketing programs to drive marketing performance improvement and begin to look at your marketing initiatives in both creative storytelling and measurable metrics.

Here are a few digital metrics and analytics for marketers to gain access to.

Website Analytics

Overview: Website analytics tools like Google Analytics offer a comprehensive view of website performance, including traffic, user behavior, and conversion metrics.

Examples:

- Traffic Metrics: Page views, unique visitors, sessions, bounce rates.
- User Behavior: Click-through rates (CTRs), time on page, navigation paths.
- Conversion Tracking: Goals achieved, conversion rates, attribution models.

- Acquisition Channels: Source/medium, referral traffic, organic vs. paid traffic.
- Site Performance: Loading times, server response, error rates.

Social Media Analytics

Overview: Social media platforms provide insights into audience engagement, demographics, content performance, and reach.

Examples:

- Engagement Metrics: Likes, comments, shares, retweets.
- Audience Demographics: Age, gender, location, interests.
- Content Performance: Top-performing posts, reach, Impressions.
- Conversion Tracking: Clicks to website, sign-ups, purchases.
- Influencer Impact: Metrics tied to influencer campaigns, reach, engagement uplift.

Email Marketing Analytics

Overview: Email marketing platforms offer insights into campaign performance, open rates, click-throughs, and subscriber behavior.

Examples:

- Open and Click Rates: Percentage of recipients who opened and engaged with emails.
- Conversion Tracking: Conversions attributed to email campaigns.

- Bounce and Unsubscribe Rates: Metrics indicating email delivery issues or disengaged audiences.
- A/B Testing Results: Performance comparisons of different email elements.
- Subscriber Behavior: Preferences, segmentation, and engagement patterns.

PPC (Pay-Per-Click) Analytics

Overview: PPC platforms like Google Ads provide data on ad performance, keywords, and audience targeting.

Examples:

- Click-Through Rate (CTR): Ratio of clicks to impressions.
- Conversion Tracking: Conversions attributed to PPC ads.
- Cost per Acquisition (CPA): Cost per conversion or action.
- Quality Score: Relevance and performance of keywords and ads.
- Keyword Performance: Clicks, impressions, and conversions per keyword.

SEO (Search Engine Optimization) Analytics

Overview: SEO tools offer insights into website visibility, keyword rankings, and organic search performance.

Examples:

- Keyword Rankings: Position in search engine results pages (SERPs).

- Organic Traffic Metrics: Traffic from search engines, new vs. returning visitors.
- Backlink Analysis: Quantity, quality, and authority of inbound links.
- Site Audit Metrics: Technical SEO insights, crawl errors, site health.
- Competitor Analysis: Benchmarking against competitor SEO strategies.
- Leveraging Analytics for Improved Marketing Performance

Data-Driven Decision Making

Overview: Marketers use analytics to make informed decisions and optimize strategies based on real-time data insights.

Examples:

- Content Optimization: Using website and social media analytics to tailor content to audience preferences.
- Ad Spend Allocation: Allocating budget to PPC or social media ads based on performance metrics.
- Campaign Iteration: Adjusting email marketing content based on open and click rates.
- Identifying High-Performing Channels: Focusing efforts on channels driving the most conversions.
- SEO Strategy Refinement: Modifying website content based on keyword and SEO analytics.

Personalization and Targeting

Overview: Utilizing analytics to create personalized experiences and targeted campaigns for specific audience segments.

Examples:

- Segmentation: Using email marketing analytics to segment audiences based on behavior or demographics for personalized campaigns.
- Dynamic Content: Tailoring website content or ads based on user behavior and preferences.
- Customized Offers: Crafting offers or promotions based on past purchases or browsing history.
- Social Media Targeting: Using insights to target specific demographics with tailored messaging.
- Retargeting Strategies: Leveraging website and social media analytics for retargeting campaigns.

Optimizing Conversion Paths

Overview: Analyzing user behavior to optimize website and marketing funnels for improved conversions.

Examples:

- Conversion Funnel Analysis: Identifying drop-off points in the customer journey and optimizing those steps.
- A/B Testing: Testing different variations of ads, emails, or landing pages to identify the most effective versions.

- CTA Optimization: Using insights to refine call-to-action elements for better engagement.
- User Experience Enhancement: Improving website usability based on navigation and behavior analytics.
- Mobile Optimization: Optimizing for mobile devices based on traffic and engagement metrics.

ROI Measurement and Attribution

Overview: Using analytics to track and attribute marketing efforts to tangible business outcomes and calculate return on investment.

Examples:

- Attribution Models: Understanding which touchpoints contribute most to conversions.
- Multi-Channel Attribution: Assessing the impact of multiple channels in the customer journey.
- LTV (Lifetime Value) Analysis: Understanding the long-term value of acquired customers.
- Cost-Benefit Analysis: Evaluating the effectiveness of different marketing channels in relation to costs.
- Campaign Performance Assessment: Measuring actual revenue or leads generated by specific campaigns.

Continuous Improvement Through Analysis

Overview: Establishing a cycle of analysis, optimization, and learning to continuously refine marketing strategies.

Examples:

- Regular Reporting and Analysis: Conducting routine analysis of various metrics to identify trends and opportunities.
- Benchmarking and Goal Setting: Setting achievable benchmarks based on historical data and industry standards.
- Staying Agile: Adapting strategies based on real-time analytics to respond to changing market dynamics.
- Learning from Failures: Analyzing unsuccessful campaigns to understand what went wrong and avoid similar mistakes.
- Staying Updated: Keeping abreast of new analytics tools and methodologies to refine strategies continually.

Made in United States
Cleveland, OH
27 February 2025